Culture and
Customs of
Ecuador

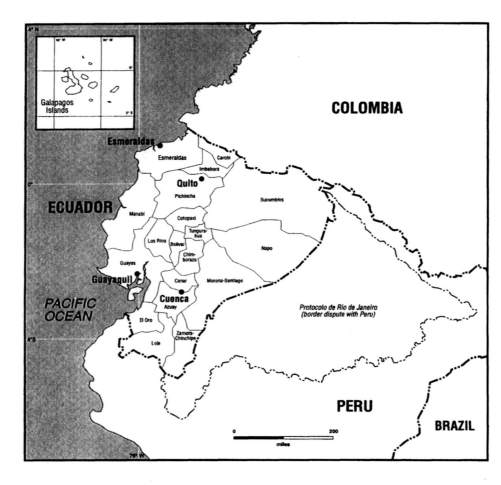

COLOMBIA

Galapagos
Islands

Esmeraldas

Esmeraldas

Carchi

Imbabura

Quito

Pichincha

ECUADOR

Sucumbios

Manabi

Cotopaxi

Tungura-
hua

Napo

Los Rios

Bolivar

Chim-
borazo

Guayas

Guayaquil

Canar

Morona-Santiago

Cuenca

Azuay

PACIFIC
OCEAN

El Oro

Zamora-
Chinchipe

Loja

Protocolo de Rio de Janeiro
(border dispute with Peru)

PERU

BRAZIL

0   200

miles

Culture and Customs of Ecuador

Michael Handelsman

Culture and Customs of Latin America and the Caribbean
Peter Standish, Series Editor

GREENWOOD PRESS
Westport, Connecticut • London

Library of Congress Cataloging-in-Publication Data

Handelsman, Michael, 1948–
    Culture and customs of Ecuador / Michael Handelsman.
        p.   cm.—(Culture and customs of Latin America and the
    Caribbean, ISSN 1521–8856)
    Includes bibliographical references and index.
    ISBN 0–313–30244–8 (alk. paper)
    1. Ecuador—Civilization—20th century.   2. Arts, Modern—20th
century—Ecuador.   3. Arts, Ecuadorian.   4. Ecuador—Social life and
customs.   5. Popular culture—Ecuador.   I. Title.   II. Series.
F3738.H34   2000
986.607′4—dc21   99–43519

British Library Cataloguing in Publication Data is available.

Library of Congress Catalog Card Number: 99–43519
ISBN: 0–313–30244–8
ISSN: 1521–8856

First published in 2000

Greenwood Press, 88 Post Road West, Westport, CT 06881
An imprint of Greenwood Publishing Group, Inc.
www.greenwood.com

Printed in the United States of America

∞

The paper used in this book complies with the
Permanent Paper Standard issued by the National
Information Standards Organization (Z39.48–1984).

10 9 8

Contents

Illustrations

Series Foreword

"CULTURE" is a problematic word. In everyday language we tend to use it in at least two senses. On the one hand we speak of cultured people and places full of culture, uses that imply a knowledge or presence of certain forms of behavior or of artistic expression that are socially prestigious. In this sense large cities and prosperous people tend to be seen as the most cultured. On the other hand, there is an interpretation of "culture" that is broader and more anthropological; culture in this broader sense refers to whatever traditions, beliefs, customs, and creative activities characterize a given community—in short, it refers to what makes that community different from others. In this second sense, everyone has culture; indeed, it is impossible to be without culture.

The problems associated with the idea of culture have been exacerbated in recent years by two trends: less respectful use of language and a greater blurring of cultural differences. Nowadays, "culture" often means little more than behavior, attitude, or atmosphere. We hear about the culture of the boardroom, of the football team, of the marketplace; there are books with titles like *The Culture of War* by Richard Gabriel (Greenwood, 1990) and *The Culture of Narcissism* by Christopher Lasch (1979). In fact, as Christopher Clausen points out in an article published in the *American Scholar* (Summer 1996), we have gotten ourselves into trouble by using the term so sloppily.

People who study culture generally assume that culture (in the anthropological sense) is learned, not genetically determined. Another general assumption made in these days of multiculturalism has been that cultural differences should be respected rather than put under pressure to change. But these assumptions, too, have sometimes proved to be problematic. For instance, multiculturalism is a fine ideal, but in practice it is not always easy to reconcile with the beliefs of the very people who advocate it: for example, is female circumcision an issue of human rights or just a different cultural practice?

The blurring of cultural differences is a process that began with the steamship, increased with radio, and is now racing ahead with the Internet. We are becoming globally homogenized. Since the English-speaking world (and the United States in particular) is the dominant force behind this process of homogenization, it behooves us to make efforts to understand the sensibilities of members of other cultures.

This series of books, a contribution toward that greater understanding, deals with the neighbors of the United States, with people who have just as much right to call themselves Americans. What are the historical, institutional, religious, and artistic features that make up the modern culture of such peoples as the Haitians, the Chileans, the Jamaicans, and the Guatemalans? How are their habits and assumptions different from our own? What can we learn from them? As we familiarize ourselves with the ways of other countries, we come to see our own from a new perspective.

Each volume in the series focuses on a single country. With slight variations to accommodate national differences, each begins by outlining the historical, political, ethnic, geographical, and linguistic context, as well as the religious and social customs, and then proceeds to a discussion of a variety of artistic activities, including the press, the media, the cinema, music, literature, and the visual and performing arts. The authors are all intimately acquainted with the countries concerned: some were born or brought up in them, and each has a professional commitment to enhancing the understanding of the culture in question.

We are inclined to suppose that our ways of thinking and behaving are normal. And so they are . . . for us. We all need to realize that ours is only one culture among many, and that it is hard to establish by any rational criteria that ours as a whole is any better (or worse) than any other. As individual members of our immediate community, we know that we must learn to respect our differences from each other. Respect for differences between cultures is no less vital. This is particularly true of the United States, a nation of immigrants that sometimes seems to be bent on destroying variety at home, and, worse still, on having others follow suit. By learning about other people's cultures, we come to understand and respect them; we earn their respect for us; and, not least, we see ourselves in a new light.

Peter Standish
East Carolina University

Acknowledgments

Having a book published is a collective process. I am indebted to my daughter, Leah, whose suggestions upon reading the first draft of each chapter were invaluable as I selected and organized the book's content. My previous department head at the University of Tennessee, John Romeiser, granted the initial approval for reducing my teaching load in Spring 1999, and thus, I was able to complete the original manuscript in a timely fashion. I am grateful to the Greenwood Publishing Group team of Wendi Schnaufer (Acquisitions Editor), Lisa Webber (Production Editor), and Beth Wilson (Copy Editor) for their many insightful comments about the most effective ways to analyze and discuss the culture and customs of Ecuador. As always, my wife, Toya, and daughter, Alysa, were a constant source of encouragement.

Finally, I wish to acknowledge that this book was to have been written originally by Dick Gerdes, professor and chair of foreign languages at George Mason University. After his wife, Aída, died tragically in Ecuador in 1997, Dick decided against writing the book and graciously recommended me for the project. I offer this volume in honor of Aída's memory and as a humble expression of friendship to Dick, *amigo y compañero*.

Introduction

Within the diverse family of Latin American nations, Ecuador is a paragon of physical contrasts and different cultures. Sandwiched between Colombia to the north and Peru to the south on the Pacific coast of South America, Ecuador sits on the equator at 0° latitude and is crossed longitudinally by the Andes Mountains. Characterized by steamy tropical jungles, snowcapped volcanoes, and all of the other climates one would expect to find between these two geographical extremes, Ecuador defies every stereotype or generalization used to describe it.

The richness of Ecuador's diverse geography is reflected by an equally diverse population. Blacks, Indians, mestizos (of mixed Indian and white blood), Asians, Europeans, and Middle Easterners constitute a multicultural mosaic that has made Ecuador a vibrant microcosm of Latin America and of the rest of the world. Within its borders, one encounters the African sounds of the marimba and the bongo drums in the northwest coastal province of Esmeraldas, the Andean flute that evokes Incan times, the Spanish guitar that symbolizes almost 500 years of Hispanic influence, herbal medicinal practices from the Amazon jungle that bring alive a pre-Columbian past, Chinese food (commonly referred to as *chifa*), and surnames such as Mahuad, Adoum, and Bucaram that have the ring of faraway places. It is no wonder that Ecuadorian historian Jorge Salvador Lara delighted in praising his country for straddling the equator and for existing in two hemispheres simultaneously while breathing in all of the planet's breezes (17).

Cultural diversity is not without conflict, however. As Ecuador's indigenous and Black communities insist on their ancestral and territorial rights within national borders, traditional notions of a unified nation with an unmistakable sense of nationality are brought into question. Indeed, ethnic and racial activists, especially since 1985, have vehemently rejected Ecuador's national mestizo myth. Rather than a harmonious integration of Indian and European cultures, Indians and Blacks contend that *mestizaje* (the mixture of Indian and white) has been a mere smokescreen for political domination and exclusion by self-proclaimed whites.

Although the 1998 National Assembly recommended that the country's constitution define Ecuador as a *país plurinacional* (a plurinational country), the debate over ethnicity and nationalism continues to provoke passionate responses. Heated discussions about loyalty, allegiance, patriotism, and civic responsibility fill the daily newspapers while Ecuadorians struggle to come to terms with their diversity. To the extent that *mestizaje* was the bedrock of the modern Ecuadorian state which was created in the nineteenth century, one might argue that the (pluri)national model of multiculturalism at the close of the twentieth century is the nucleus of a postmodern Ecuador.

Ecuador's identity issues highlight the country's relevance to understanding many of the world's ethnic and racial conflicts. At the same time, however, Ecuador and its history are clearly representative of much of Latin American history and development from pre-Columbian times to the present. Although most readers have traditionally overlooked Ecuador when studying Latin America, judging the country's place among Latin American nations primarily in terms of its small size and population, this volume argues for the centrality of the Ecuadorian experience vis-à-vis such topics as the Spanish conquest, colonization, the wars of independence, economic dependence, border disputes, the tensions between tradition and change, and the social costs common to boom-and-bust economies. In effect, Ecuador is a laboratory located at the center of the world where attentive readers will discover the close interplay that exists between its unique history and the heritage it shares with the rest of Latin America.

The chapters that compose this volume are a tribute to the diversity and vitality of a small country that the Ecuadorian statesman and writer Leopoldo Benites Vinueza described in the title of a book as a land of "drama and paradox." Ecuador is an ecological, geographical, and cultural haven of seemingly infinite resources next to pockets of extreme poverty and injustice typical of the Third World. Yet the spirit of Ecuadorians continues to be resilient and unbroken. Amid devastation by natural catastrophes or political and economic corruption, and despite the many setbacks suffered throughout their history, Ecuadorians continue their quest for solutions with unflinching resolve. Read within this context, the culture and customs of Ecuador described in this volume should be a catalyst for further study and understanding of a small, but complex and inspiring country.

REFERENCES

Benites Vinueza, Leopoldo. *Ecuador: Drama y paradoja.* Quito: Banco Central del Ecuador y Corporación Editora Nacional, 1986.
Lara, Jorge Salvador. *Breve historia contemporánea del Ecuador.* Mexico City: Fondo de Cultura Económica, 1994.

Chronology

12000 B.C.	Archaeologists believe the first signs of human populations appear in present-day Ecuador.
1460	The Inca leader Túpac Yupanqui begins to expand his empire into the northern Andes.
1525	The Inca Huayna Capac dies; his sons Huáscar (from Cuzco, Peru) and Atahualpa (from Quito, Ecuador), who have different mothers, wage a civil war in 1532 to determine who will succeed their father. This civil war fragments the Inca empire, and thus facilitates the Spanish conquest of the region. The dispute between the two brothers, which Atahualpa wins, is considered to be an early manifestation of later border disputes between Ecuador and Peru.
1531	The Spaniard Francisco Pizarro arrives with his soldiers. They capture Atahualpa in 1532 and demand a ransom of gold for his release.
1533	The Spanish conquerors kill Atahualpa and begin to consolidate their control over the region.
1534	Quito is officially founded by the Spanish conquerors, who defeat Rumiñuahi, the last Inca general to resist Spanish domination.

1535   On July 25, Guayaquil is formally founded by Francisco de
          Orellana; it will be one of Spain's principal seaports along the
          Pacific coast. During the late seventeenth century, Guayaquil
          is a popular target for English pirates.

1541   Gonzalo Pizarro and Francisco de Orellana depart from Quito
          to explore the Amazon region, which, according to legend, is
          the location of El Dorado, a land of unlimited riches. Orellana
          travels the length of the Amazon River during this expedition.

1547   The first Catholic bishop assumes office in Quito. During the
          sixteenth and seventeenth centuries, Quito becomes a major
          center for the Catholic Church in Latin America; some of the
          continent's most spectacular colonial and baroque churches are
          built there.

1563   Spain officially establishes the Royal Audiencia (Royal Circuit
          Court) of Quito, converting present-day Ecuador into one of
          Spain's key colonial administrative centers.

1592   Local mestizos and creoles (American-born people of Spanish
          heritage) stage an uprising against the Spanish Crown to pro-
          test taxation and other colonial controls. The uprising, called
          the Revolution of the Alcabalas (sales tax), is frequently seen
          as an early prelude to the independence movement of the nine-
          teenth century.

1718   The Spanish Crown abolishes the Royal Audiencia of Quito,
          and the affected territory is placed under the administrative
          supervision of the Viceroyalty of Santa Fe de Bogotá in present-
          day Colombia.

1722   The Spanish Crown reestablishes the Royal Audiencia of Quito
          in 1720 but places it under the administrative charge of the
          Viceroyalty of Peru in 1722.

1736   A team of scientists from the Academy of Sciences in Paris
          arrives in Quito to measure the equator. The results determine
          the exact shape of the Earth and profoundly influence the fu-
          ture of cartography, geography, geophysics, astronomy, and the
          natural sciences. This scientific mission continued until 1743.

1739   The Spanish Crown once again changes the administrative status of the Royal Audiencia of Quito by moving it from the jurisdiction of the Viceroyalty of Peru to that of the Viceroyalty of Santa Fe de Bogotá.

1767   The king of Spain expels the Jesuits from Spain and all of its territories. The Jesuits had established themselves as a dominant force within Ecuador, particularly through their leading role in education and their development of a profitable agricultural system. Many consider the expulsion of the Jesuits to have been a major setback for Ecuador's cultural and educational programs.

1792   The first newspaper appears in Quito, under the direction of Eugenio de Santa Cruz y Espejo. The editor and his paper, *Primicias de la cultura de Quito* (The First Fruits of Culture from Quito), prepared the way for Ecuador's independence movement, which began formally in 1809.

1809   On August 10 a group of Ecuadorian creoles depose the Spanish government and declare a sovereign junta. Spanish military forces from Lima and Bogotá react quickly, and the junta is forced to relinquish its power because of inadequate resources. Despite promises that there will be no reprisals, the junta leaders are imprisoned. On August 2, 1810, they are massacred in prison. The Quito massacre becomes a clarion for independence leaders from throughout South America. Simón Bolívar refers to the tragedy in his 1813 declaration of war against Spain.

1812   The first constitution of an independent Quito is written.

1820   On October 9 and November 3, Guayaquil and Cuenca, respectively, declare their independence and formally join the independence movement.

1822   Ecuador wins independence on May 24 when Marshal Antonio José de Sucre leads the revolutionary armies in the defeat of the Spanish forces at the Battle of Pichincha. Ecuador is annexed by Gran Colombia, which consists of Venezuela, Colombia, and Ecuador.

1830   On May 13 the District of the South (consisting of three principal regions called *intendencias*: Quito, Guayaquil, and Cuenca) breaks with Gran Colombia to form an independent state that takes the name Ecuador (equator).

1832   Ecuador takes possession of the Galápagos Islands.

1858   War breaks out between Ecuador and Peru over territorial limits. Peru imposes a naval blockade.

1860   Gabriel García Moreno seizes power; he is elected president in 1861 by the National Assembly, and the military conflict with Peru ends.

1895   On June 5, General Eloy Alfaro initiates the Liberal Revolution. Most Ecuadorians agree that this historic event marks the beginning of modern-day Ecuador.

1922   On November 15 a general workers' strike in Guayaquil ends in a bloody massacre by government forces. This tragic event will greatly influence Ecuador's social and political scene for the rest of the twentieth century, especially with respect to labor unions and the growth of socialism.

1924   Anglo-Ecuadorian Oilfields Limited discovers oil on Ecuador's coast.

1941   Ecuador and Peru are again at war over their territorial sovereignty. The war ends in defeat for Ecuador.

1944   Under the leadership of Benjamín Carrión, during the presidency of José María Velasco Ibarra, Casa de la Cultura Ecuatoriana, the independent House of Ecuadorian Culture, charged with promoting the arts and sciences at all levels of society, is founded. Its traveling libraries and educational radio programs have contributed to raising Ecuador's literacy rates; its sponsorship of arts and crafts festivals has brought greater visibility to local artisans and their work; its financial support for Ecuadorian artists has played a decisive role in the artistic success of such renowned painters as Oswaldo Guayasamín and Eduardo Kingman; and its scholarly exchange and lecture programs have attempted to advance knowledge in science and technology.

| 1945 | Ecuador joins the United Nations. |

1948   Galo Plaza Lasso becomes president and initiates a period of peace and prosperity arising especially from the beginning of Ecuador's banana boom. Despite periodic slumps in production and export earnings, Ecuador has remained one of the world's leading banana producers.

1967   Texaco-Gulf makes a major oil discovery in Ecuador's Amazon region. By the early 1970s Ecuador becomes a major oil exporter and enters a period of economic prosperity, accelerated urbanization, and modernization.

1972   The military ousts President Velasco Ibarra and establishes a military government. Despite unprecedented profits from oil exports, much of the national wealth is squandered through inefficiency and corruption.

1979   After seven years of a military government, Ecuador returns to constitutional rule and, in a democratic election, chooses Jaime Roldós as president. Strife within Roldós's political party and within the Congress frustrates many of his reformist programs.

1981   President Roldós dies in a plane crash on May 24; Vice President Osvaldo Hurtado assumes the presidency and heads a government that will be tremendously hampered by the nation's foreign debt.

1986   Birth of Confederación de Nacionalidades Indígenas del Ecuador (CONAIE; Confederation of Indigenous Nationalities of Ecuador); it brings together Indians from the Coast, Sierra, and Oriente regions to defend and promote Indian land rights, religion, and culture.

1990   Indigenous groups and sympathizers throughout Ecuador stage a massive protest on June 4; the government receives 16 proposals that address issues ranging from land reform to redefining Ecuador as a *estado plurinacional*. For the first time in their history, many Ecuadorians acknowledge that the country's diverse indigenous population constitutes a major force in national politics.

1997   On February 5 some 2 million Ecuadorians peacefully take to the streets throughout the country and demand the resignation of President Abdalá Bucaram because of his corrupt and ineffective government. Bucaram leaves the country, and the peaceful nature of the protest is hailed as a major victory for democracy. In 1997, under interim President Fabián Alarcón, Ecuador elects a National Assembly charged with rewriting the constitution and preparing for new elections.

1998   Jamil Mahuad becomes Ecuador's president on August 10; he signs a peace accord with Peru on October 26.

1

Context

Ecuador is a small country about the size of Colorado and has approximately 12 million inhabitants, 60 percent of whom live in cities. The country is divided into three basic regions: the Pacific Coast; the Andes Mountains, referred to as the Sierra, and the Amazon region, or Oriente, that lies east of the Andes. In addition, the Galápagos Islands belong to Ecuador. Located 1,000 kilometers west of mainland Ecuador in the Pacific Ocean, they have been referred to as the "Enchanted Islands." It was there that Charles Darwin did much of the research that would lead to his theory of evolution.

Ecuador has long been a favorite of foreign tourists and travelers for its diverse geography, majestic scenery, varied flora and fauna, and rich cultural traditions. Moreover, in contrast to the turbulent conditions so often characteristic of Ecuador's neighbors—Colombia to the north and Peru to the south—Ecuador is basically a peaceful country known for its hospitality to visitors.

This chapter identifies the context within which Ecuador has evolved, especially since 1822, when it won political independence from Spain. Rather than offer an exhaustive list of historical events the following pages treat selected topics that might be called defining moments and issues. Because these topics are an expression of the ongoing tensions and conflicts of a people, their influence is felt constantly in one form or another, demonstrating that history is never static or fixed in some lost era. Moreover, the Ecuadorian case clearly illustrates the degree to which all countries are projects in the making and, as such, require continuous study and reflection.

THE POLITICS AND LANGUAGE OF NATIONAL IDENTITY

With the birth of the Latin American republics at the beginning of the nineteenth century, intellectuals in each country initiated their search for a national, and sometimes a continental, identity. Attempts to express clearly each nation's uniqueness and specificity were necessary to complete political independence from Spain. Unfortunately, such a project of self-definition proved to be elusive and deceptive. Primarily concerned with establishing political unity and social order for their respective countries, many of the early interpreters created concepts of nationhood that were a reflection of a privileged ruling class's self-image: European, Roman Catholic, and Spanish-speaking. Thus, concepts of "Ecuadorianness" tended to exclude Indians and Blacks, converting a deeply heterogeneous society into an imagined nation similar to what Benedict Anderson describes in his book *Imagined Communities: Reflections on the Origin and Spread of Nationalism.*

The rhetoric of nationhood, with its attendant notions of patriotism and nationalism, poses a challenge to anyone interested in learning about Ecuador. Because one person's fiction is another's reality, one might say that Ecuador is made up of many Ecuadors. Clearly, the disparities between the Ecuadors are the result of conflicting agendas that make up much of the country's social history. The conquerors against the conquered, the powerful against the powerless, the literate against the illiterate, the rich against the poor, and the ruling elite against the masses exemplify, in one fashion or another, a continuous clash of cultures in which the mastery of language has determined whose version of history would prevail.

These dichotomies represent extremes and may appear to understate Ecuador's complexity; such dualistic reasoning, however, is an expression of the deep conflicts that are at the very center of Ecuadorian identity. Certainly, a definition of Ecuador lies somewhere between its being a nation beset by poverty and exploitation, on the one hand, and a nation once described as *"una pequeña gran nación"* (a small great nation) (Carrión 166), on the other. The use of language, especially written language, is at the heart of each interpretation. Indeed, with the arrival in 1531 of the Spanish conquerors led by Francisco Pizarro, the country's history would emerge as a struggle for power whose victors would become the masters of language. As such, they would impose their versions of history and "truth."

The struggle over language was, indeed, at the heart of the clash between Atahualpa, the last Incan leader, and Father Vicente de Valverde, the Spanish priest who accompanied Pizarro and directed efforts to convert the Indians to Christianity. The Incas, who had an oral culture, initially resisted the conversion efforts through use of the Bible. After Valverde held up the Bible and told Atahualpa that it contained the word of God, Atahualpa put the Good Book to his ear. When he did not hear anything, he defiantly threw the Bible to the ground in disgust. Shortly after, Atahualpa was executed, and from the Spaniards' victory came the domination of a culture that consolidated its power through the written word.

The story about Atahualpa and Father Valverde not only captures the inevitable tensions that characterize societies made up of diverse cultures and divergent interests; it also evokes the legacy of Atahualpa's defiance. Through the centuries such pride and resistance have served, consciously or subconsciously, as a catalyst for cultural survival and ethnic affirmation in a nation where, paradoxically, many of its histories have been strategically written as a means of denying and covering up the country's non-European heritage.

Throughout its history Ecuador has known many Atahualpas and Father Valverdes. Their original confrontation has been played out repeatedly, and although the names and circumstances have varied, language as a source of power and privilege has been a constant force that continues to affect Ecuadorians and their attempts to define themselves while forging a national destiny. Much of the current debate over Ecuador's national identity hinges on the use and interpretation of fundamental phrases and traditional terminology vis-à-vis the *nation*. It would be a serious mistake to view the struggle over language as gratuitous. Too many Ecuadorians have fought and died in wars and revolts that, at some level, were provoked by the need to control language and self-definition. The right to defend Ecuador as a *"país amazónico"* (a country whose boundaries include parts of the Amazon basin) has had international implications, as evidenced by numerous armed conflicts over territorial rights and boundaries between Ecuador and Peru. The notion that Ecuador is a *"país andino"* (an Andean country) has frequently led to internal strife; the country's non-Andean regions have denounced political centralization as a form of privilege and a source of disenfranchisement. Finally, defining Ecuador as a *"país plurinacional"* (a country made up of many nations) is really about human rights, and consequently large segments of society (the real and symbolic descendants of Atahualpa) have called for the restructuring of traditional forms of government and governmental jurisdiction. In short, the original struggle between Atahualpa and Father Valverde did not end with the Inca's death in 1533.

The monument marking the center of the world at the equator. Courtesy of James Minton.

Ecuador: An Imaginary Name for an Imaginary Place

Ecuador's name is Spanish for "equator," which a group of scientists, led by the French mathematician Charles de La Condamine, charted between 1736 and 1743 near Quito. Unlike most Latin American countries, whose names evoke a concrete reference to history or a prominent geographical feature that people acknowledge as central to identifying the uniqueness of their nation, Ecuador's name has proven to be much more problematic. Logically, Ecuador should be called Quito, the name of the country's capital. In fact, the Incas referred to present-day Ecuador as Quitu. After the Conquest, Spain adopted the name of Quito, creating the Royal Audiencia of Quito in 1563.

Unfortunately for Ecuador, during three centuries of colonial rule, Spain waffled numerous times on deciding exactly where the region belonged within the administrative and bureaucratic structure of its colonies. At the time of the Conquest, which occurred during the first half of the sixteenth century, the Spanish government placed Ecuador under the immediate jurisdiction of the Viceroyalty of Peru; in the eighteenth century, Ecuador was assigned to the Viceroyalty of Santa Fe de Bogotá in 1718, reassigned to Peru in 1722, and finally was returned to Bogotá's administrative control in 1739. As Spain altered the lines of demarcation between its colonies, the integrity of Quito as a fixed and unified place was fragmented. Shifting boundaries and allegiances gave rise to new districts called *intendencias*, one of which was called Quito.

Once again, language would play a decisive role in determining Ecuador's fate. The administrative realignments and the ambiguity that eventually characterized its original name (*audiencia, intendencia*, or both) brought endless territorial disputes, particularly with regard to its elusive, and seemingly illusory, national boundaries with Colombia and, above all, Peru. Armed confrontations with the latter in 1910, 1941, 1981, and 1995, and the endless legal battles over related international matters, have drained Ecuador of vital resources and time that might have been better spent on modernization and development. Defending territorial sovereignty, however, cannot be taken lightly, especially when it has to do with establishing rights over such strategic natural resources as oil.

It is ironic just how appropriate Ecuador's name has become, at least in a symbolic sense. Despite claims by many Ecuadorian intellectuals that Quito was the most logical choice of name for the republic due to its long history, and that being identified with the equator did not set Ecuador apart from the many other countries similarly located, the name does capture much of the drama and paradox that have deeply affected the country throughout its history. An imaginary name for an imaginary place. The equator does not really exist; it is a mathematical concept conceived (imagined) by scientists! Because Ecuador's borders have changed so often, it would appear that all of its demarcations—geographical as well as symbolic—have been subjected to the capriciousness of the imagined.

In the context of colonialism and other forms of external domination that are so often an integral part of Third World countries, Ecuador's search for identity has been especially intense and urgent. Affirmations of "Ecuadorianness," whether declared in public forums or written in literature, have frequently been part of a long-term struggle to counter a national image that many foreigners have rarely taken seriously. In a sense, Ecuador as a concept, as an "imagined community," too often has suggested an *absence* of meaning, and from that state of confusion has arisen the need to understand Ecuadorian national identity as a search for stability and legitimacy.

The Small Great Nation

In 1941, the Peruvian army crossed into Ecuador, and within a matter of days reaffirmed its rights over more than 200,000 square kilometers of Ecuadorian territory in the Amazon region. A group of mediators consisting of Argentina, Brazil, Chile, and the United States was formed, and a settlement called the Protocolo de Río de Janeiro was reached in 1942. For Ecuadorians, the agreement was a solution imposed upon them by an international community that was primarily concerned with World War II; thus, Ecuador's territorial rights were sacrificed in the name of peace. Ecuadorians viewed the military and diplomatic defeats of 1941–1942 as a source of national shame. On the one hand, they denounced their government's inability to guarantee national security; on the other hand, they resented the ease with which the international community accepted yet another reconfiguration of Ecuador's boundaries.

Indeed, one would be hard pressed to identify events in the twentieth century that have provoked more debate and affected Ecuador's social, political, and economical landscape more deeply than the 1941 war with Peru. The entire second half of the century is full of attempts to renegotiate the *Protocolo* and to reclaim what Ecuador considers to be its rightful place in the contested Amazonian region. Unfortunately, the intense feelings Ecuadorians have about their national sovereignty and national integrity have made many of them easy prey to political manipulation and xenophobic propaganda. Urgent problems such as poverty, unemployment, and political corruption have too often been tolerated by Ecuadorians as politicians have distracted them with appeals to their nationalism and patriotism. In addition, the constant threat of armed conflicts with Peru has led governments to spend enormous amounts of money on the military; consequently, ongoing financial investment in desperately needed social programs has suffered greatly.

In light of the far-reaching consequences of the 1941 war with Peru, it is no wonder that such prominent Ecuadorian intellectuals as Benjamín Carrión (1897–1979) have reacted passionately to the conflict when discussing national identity. At the same time that the international community agreed to (re)write the physical maps that would (re)locate and (re)identify Ecuador for the rest of the world, Carrión set out to (re)define his country by (re)affirming Ecuador's rich traditions and its potential for future greatness among Latin American nations.

In *Cartas al Ecuador* (Letters to Ecuador), originally published in 1943, Carrión responded to the general malaise and state of demoralization that had been consuming Ecuadorians since their defeat in 1941. Skepticism and a defeatest attitude threatened to plunge the country into political, social, economic, and cultural stagnation. Carrión understood that without the general will to continue defending the country's interests or the common belief in its intrinsic value as a nation among nations, Ecuador was doomed to a kind of nonexistence, be it physical, spiritual, or both.

As Carrión urged Ecuadorians to reconnect with their past and believe in their future, he celebrated the ability of small countries like Ecuador to achieve greatness. Specifically, he asserted that although Ecuador would never be a military or economic power, it could earn respect for its cultural traditions and creativity. With that premise in mind, he evoked past glories and insisted that Ecuadorians have the courage to honor their forebears. "They took from us the fatherland we had. Now, it is imperative that we reclaim our national identity" (168; author's translation).

Some Ecuadorian intellectuals of later generations have criticized Carrión, claiming that his insistence on cultural greatness was illusory and did nothing to solve the very real problems of hunger, injustice, and economic dependency. Be that as it may, his story does illustrate the extent to which many Ecuadorians have struggled with the identity issue. Ecuadorian national identity per se has transcended purely philosophical grounds precisely because people continue to consider it a determining sociopolitical force in the country's past, present, and future.

INDEPENDENCE AND THE BIRTH OF ECUADOR

With the Wars of Independence that began in earnest in 1810, the nineteenth century became a period of national formation and consolidation throughout Latin America. Ecuador was no exception. Even after its liberation by Simón Bolívar in 1822, Ecuador was still referred to as the Distrito del Sur (the Southern District) and identified as part of Colombia. Thus, during the first years of independence from Spain, present-day Ecuador formed part of the original Gran Colombia (Greater Colombia) that included Colombia, present-day Panama, and Venezuela. Because of numerous conflicting interests among powerful social and military groups in the region, Gran Colombia broke up into three independent nations in 1830: Venezuela, Colombia (which included Panama), and Ecuador. It was only then that the name Ecuador was adopted as a kind of political compromise; in light of the deep rivalries that separated the three distinct regions that made up the Dis-

Monument honoring Simón Bolívar and José de San Martín, liberators of South America, who met at Guayaquil in 1822. Courtesy of James Minton.

trito del Sur (Quito, Cuenca, and Guayaquil), the leadership of the period considered the name Ecuador to be the most neutral choice.

Regionalism, of course, was not a new phenomenon for Ecuador, nor would it end with independence. The area's geography has contributed in no small measure to the country's lack of social and political unity. The Andes Mountains that run from north to south are divided into two principal chains which are connected by numerous mountain ranges that form valleys. Throughout the region's history, these valleys have been centers for diverse groups of people, and due to the difficult terrain, communication and unification have been problematic at best. Thus, Ecuador has long been influenced by independent-minded people whose interests have rarely transcended the natural confines of their local borders.

The legacy of geographical separation appears to have produced the intense conflicts between Guayaquil and Quito that have greatly determined national development (or lack thereof), especially since the early nineteenth century. Guayaquil is the nation's principal seaport and international trade center, while Quito has been the bastion of traditional church authority and landholding interests. Until the completion of the railroad in 1908, communication between these two cities was most difficult, and even with aviation, a modern road system, and modern technologies, Guayaquil and Quito more often than not continue to be distant rivals rather than united partners. Indeed, what were originally geographical obstacles have been replaced by social, political, economic, and cultural divisions that still prevent Ecuadorians from forging a common national project of development and unification.

Although the degree to which these two urban centers have influenced national events cannot be overestimated, the country's dividedness is much more than a "tale of two cities." In fact, many Ecuadorians have struggled to overcome the complex causes and effects of national polarization. One such Ecuadorian was Gabriel García Moreno (1821–1875), who was twice president of Ecuador (1861–1865, 1869–1875). García Moreno organized a centralized government capable of controlling and administering public resources while planning public works projects throughout the country. He established the first efficient treasury, issued a uniform currency, and was able to attract foreign investment. Under his leadership, new schools and institutes were created, and numerous institutions such as the military were reorganized and modernized. According to the historian Enrique Ayala Mora, during the García Moreno period "Ecuador became an organized country, with better communication, and with a growing level of education" (79; author's translation).

Unfortunately, such progress did not come without severe costs. According to Ayala Mora, opposition was met with some of the cruelest repression ever known to Ecuadorians (79). The contradictions that characterized García Moreno's government were logical outcomes of his being an enlightened despot: learned and ruthless.

Because he was an astute politician, García Moreno understood that the Catholic Church could be an effective source of power and control in chaotic Ecuador. Under his rule, Ecuador virtually became a theocratic state; opposition leaders and Freemasons were persecuted, and only practicing Catholics were recognized as citizens. Moreover, in 1863, García Moreno signed a concordat that gave the Catholic Church control over education and restored ecclesiastical courts; in 1873, he convinced Congress to dedicate Ecuador to the Sacred Heart of Jesus. Although García Moreno's policies seemed to be rooted in a moral and spiritual project legitimized by the divine intervention of the Catholic Church, a more complete evaluation of his government reveals a basic dilemma that has plagued Ecuador and the rest of Latin America since the early years of independence: Can there be both economic progress and social justice?

THE BEGINNINGS OF MODERN-DAY ECUADOR

In 1875, García Moreno was assassinated in front of the presidential palace, a clear indication that political order and economic progress were not enough to justify the full range of the government's policies and methods. With García Moreno's death, Ecuador once again fell into a political vacuum that favored a small, wealthy elite and its principal ally, the Catholic Church. Despite ongoing opposition from the liberals, by the end of the nineteenth century Ecuador was a deeply stratified country with a rigid class structure reminiscent of colonial times, when the clergy and the nobility wielded absolute power.

In 1895, the stage was set for a dramatic change to take place in Ecuador—the separation of church and state. The Liberal Revolution, which began on June 5, 1895, led Ecuador into the twentieth century and modernity. Under the leadership of General Eloy Alfaro, the state secularized education, civil marriage superseded the ecclesiastical ceremony, divorce became legal, freedom of religion became law, and the church lost its large landholdings. Aside from independence, the Liberal Revolution of 1895 can be seen as Ecuador's only authentic revolution in the sense of producing profound social change (Lara 422).

Since the Liberal Revolution was largely the result of economic growth and the rise of an emerging bourgeois class, new political and economic structures were essential if Ecuador was to take advantage of new capitalist ventures, especially in light of the increased foreign demand for Ecuadorian cacao (chocolate). Thus, exporters of agricultural products and neophyte capitalists from the Coast replaced the country's previous oligarchy, which was rooted in the Sierra and whose interests lay in religious and feudalist traditions.

Unfortunately, the economic prosperity enjoyed by the country's nouveaux riches derailed many of the liberal principles that inspired Alfaro and the 1895 Revolution. Bankers and exporters from the Coast, in particular, became more concerned about preserving their newly acquired power and prestige than about restructuring society. Thus, Ecuador's new power brokers fragmented Alfaro's Radical Liberal Party by creating a conservative right wing that abandoned the poor and entered into strong alliances with foreign investors and old-guard landowners. As in other Latin American countries, liberalism in Ecuador became shallow and devoid of much of its original commitment to radical social change.

Although one oligarchy (the bourgeoisie) ended up replacing another (the traditional landowners), and despite the growing trend toward economic dependency within the new economic order of international capitalism, Eloy Alfaro and the 1895 Liberal Revolution continue to symbolize the emergence of democracy and modernization in Ecuador. Under Alfaro, education reached more people than in the past, and a small middle class of merchants, artisans, and professionals slowly began to influence Ecuador's social and political landscape.

Just as García Moreno had dominated Ecuadorian politics during his period of influence (1860–1875), so Eloy Alfaro defined and shaped the course of Ecuadorian society between 1895 and 1912, the year in which he was brutally executed in Quito by a mob. Under Alfaro, Ecuador evolved from a theocratic state to a secular one; under his leadership, democracy began to make some inroads against a long-standing tradition of absolute privilege.

Because of sweeping social reforms, the Alfaro period has been characterized as one of national consolidation in which Ecuador became a more inclusive and representative country (Ayala Mora 87). Alfaro's commitment to the completion of the railroad between Quito and Guayaquil symbolized his broadly conceived agenda of integration, be it economic, political, or social. Unfortunately, as Alfaro's death suggests, Ecuador was still far from becoming a unified nation.

Despite the Revolution of 1895's shortcomings and failures, by the turn of the century, Ecuador had indeed entered a new era. To be sure, various oligarchic groups created new alliances to counter the forces of change that Alfaro had introduced. Political parties and grassroots organizations arose, however, and they began to champion the rights and needs of heretofore marginalized and disenfranchised social groups.

Workers' societies that originally were dedicated to protecting their members' welfare gradually became radicalized as Ecuador's export economy suffered major losses. Increased unemployment and unfair labor practices led to sporadic protests and strikes. By 1922 Ecuador had plunged into a general crisis that culminated in the massacre of more than 1,000 striking workers in Guayaquil on November 15. On that day, labor unions became a political force in Ecuador.

With a struggling economy and increased social tensions, Ecuadorians were ripe for new ideas. The Mexican Revolution of 1910 and the Russian Revolution of 1917 captured the imagination of numerous groups. By 1926, Ecuador had its own Socialist Party; in 1931, pro-Soviet socialists formed Ecuador's Communist Party. Whereas past political struggles were mainly between conservative and liberal elites, by 1930, Ecuadorian politics had begun to define national interests more broadly. Although true political power continued in the hands of a small minority, the needs and interests of workers and Indians, for example, could no longer be ignored.

A BOOM-AND-BUST ECONOMY

Since independence, Ecuador has moved between military or civilian dictatorships and elected governments that rarely have completed their full terms. Among the many causes of such political instability is an economy that has been equally unstable. Because Ecuador has always been primarily an exporter of raw materials, the country continues to be susceptible to the ebb and flow of international markets and prices. Cacao, bananas, and oil have determined every aspect of Ecuadorian society since the late nineteenth century.

Unlike many Latin American countries, whose economic dependency can be attributed to their being primarily exporters of one crop, such as coffee, or one natural resource, such as copper, and thus are highly vulnerable to sudden fluctuations in the conditions of supply and demand of world markets, Ecuador has been a major exporter of three different resources that might suggest a more diversified and resilient economy than those of its neighbors. Ecuadorians have frequently referred to such variety when describing their country as a paradise that has been blessed with untapped resources and wealth. Such idealized accounts come from two distinct schools of thought. On the one hand, there are those who have celebrated Ecuador's supposed uniqueness and unbounded potential for growth and development in a nationalistic discourse intended to secure a place of importance and legitimacy among Latin American nations. On the other hand, there have been Ecuadorians who have taken the "paradise" image and denounced a political and economic system that has failed to take full advantage of its opportunities. Undoubtedly, the "real" Ecuador lies somewhere between these two extremes.

Cacao

Between 1880 and 1922, cacao was Ecuador's proverbial golden egg, particularly on the Coast, where landowners cultivated it. It gave rise to the beginnings of a lucrative agro-export industry made up of growers, exporters, and bankers. Prosperity from cacao gave rise to the country's first bourgeoisie, and Guayaquil's dominance as a seaport and urban center was firmly established. In short, cacao dramatically changed Ecuador's social and political profile: the Coast's bourgeois class wrested power from the Sierra's feudal oligarchy, and as urbanization began in earnest, a small middle class emerged. Unfortunately, those who benefited most from cacao did very little to invest their resources in the country's social and economic infrastructure. Long-term projects capable of creating alternative sources of wealth and viable markets for internal consumption were rarely pursued. Cacao generated an export economy that nurtured financial speculation more than investment; the allure of foreign imports dwarfed any notion of fully developing local industry and manufacturing. By 1922, the cacao boom had become a bust; a major decrease in foreign demand and a plant fungus that devastated most of the cacao crops demonstrated just how tenuous Ecuador's economic growth had been.

Ecuador's economic woes gave rise to social tensions and conflicts. Between 1922 and 1944, Ecuador had more than 20 different governments. It was during this chaotic period that José María Velasco Ibarra (1893–1979) became Ecuador's most dominant political figure of the twentieth century. He was president or dictator five times, completing only one term without being ousted by the military (1952–1956).

Velasco was a highly charismatic and totally unpredictable caudillo (political boss). Whether he was assailing evil foreign infuences or inept national politicians, his acerbic and aggressive rhetoric always appealed to the masses, who saw him as their "Prophet." Once in office, though, Velasco aligned himself with traditional power brokers whose legacy was one of corruption rather than of civic duty. By all accounts, however, Velasco never profited financially from holding political office. He was a political zealot who believed that he was destined to be Ecuador's savior. Because of his fervor and xenophobia, his political intentions never transcended the inconsistencies and general incoherence of his public rhetoric and fanaticism. It is no wonder, then, that through the years Velasco's political party, the Partido Velasquista (the Velasco Party), could offer voters only a dynamic personality rather than a viable political platform.

Bananas and Political Stability

By the end of the 1940s, Ecuador's fortunes appeared to change for the better. Galo Plaza Lasso (1906–1987), elected president in 1948, was the first president elected since 1924 to complete a full four-year term in office. Plaza's presidency coincided with the beginning of Ecuador's second major economic boom: the production and export of bananas. As Ecuador quickly became one of the world's leading banana exporters, its newfound prosperity created an abundance of opportunities for development and modernization.

But the period's growth was not limited to exports. By 1950, in addition to a general resurgence in agricultural development, there was the rise of middle-class groups associated with the production and export of bananas as well as with the public and private service sectors of the economy (Ayala Mora 98–99).

With economic prosperity came political stability. Three successive governments were freely elected (1948, 1952, and 1956), and each president completed his term including Velasco, who won the presidency in 1952. Galo Plaza set the tone for this period. Educated in the United States, he was the son of an ex-president and diplomat, and understood the workings of international funding agencies. During his presidency, foreign investment grew and Ecuador's currency was one of the most stable in Latin America. Plaza balanced the national budget, serviced the public debt, and strengthened the treasury with increased reserves.

By the end of the 1950s, however, the economic pendulum had swung again, plunging Ecuador into political and economic turmoil. Ecuador's success with bananas helped create a highly competitive banana export industry throughout Central America, Asia, and Africa. With the increased competition, the international economic forces of supply and demand created unbalanced budgets, currency devaluations, public discontent, and political unrest in Ecuador.

In 1960, Velasco Ibarra once again won the presidency by exploiting public discontent through demagoguery. During his campaign, he publicly repudiated the Protocolo de Río de Janeiro, the international agreement that had favored Peruvian interests over those of Ecuador after the 1941 war, thereby reopening old nationalist wounds. Moreover, in light of the 1959 Cuban Revolution and the subsequent resurgence of leftist movements throughout the Americas, Velasco Ibarra appealed to the masses with his anti-imperialist and anti-United States rhetoric. Unfortunately, a deteriorating economy proved to be too much for Ecuador's "Prophet." Internal political strife, especially between Velasco and his vice president, quickly led to Velasco's ouster in 1961.

After two years of chaos, the military took over the government in 1963 and remained in power until 1966. Economic prosperity again proved to be tenuous. The end of Ecuador's second economic bonanza was not, however, a mere return to past conditions. The banana export crisis and the general tenor of the 1960s opened the way to a turbulent process of modernization and social reform marked by rapid urban growth, the development and increasing accessibility of radio and television, and the Catholic Church's renewed commitment to the poor (Ayala Mora 102).

Oil and National Euphoria

The military junta that held power between 1963 and 1966 responded to Ecuador's deepening crisis with repression. Despite some reforms, especially agrarian reform, its principal legacy was a National Security Act that gave the government a free hand in squelching all forms of opposition that might be associated with Fidel Castro and his sympathizers. Repression was met with massive resistance and civil disobedience. National strikes by workers and students, public demonstrations, and a general unwillingness to accept the political status quo sounded the junta's death knell.

During a period of transition, two interim presidents took charge of the government until full-scale elections could be held in 1968. Velasco Ibarra became president for a fifth time. The period's political and economic turbulence were unmanageable, however, and in 1970, Velasco Ibarra disbanded Congress and declared himself dictator. He was deposed by the military in 1972.

The military government assumed power precisely when Ecuador became a major exporter of oil. Under the leadership of Guillermo Rodríguez Lara, Ecuador joined the world's other major oil producers by becoming a member of OPEC in 1973. The government defended Ecuador's sovereignty over its natural resources, and little by little, it displaced Texaco-Gulf in the production and sale of Ecuador's oil. At a time when international oil prices reached an all-time high, Ecuador saw unprecedented profits fill its national treasury. With their newly acquired prosperity, many Ecuadorians accepted the military's claim that Ecuador's government was "nationalist" and "revolutionary."

Despite the unparalleled growth and modernization that characterized the 1970s, much of Ecuador's progress proved to be more imagined than real. Poor planning, widespread corruption, and continued dependence on foreign markets constituted the makings of yet another economic bust. According to one market analyst:

Since 1972, Ecuador has gone through one of the most significant periods of economic growth in her history, yet, so far, this growth has brought little benefit to the average Ecuadorian. The development which has occurred has mainly been "incrementalist" rather than "transformationist," continuing and accentuating past trends, rather than achieving radical changes in the social and economic structure. Unearned windfalls rarely bring great happiness, and Ecuador's oil wealth is no exception to this rule. (R. J. Bromley, in Martz 389–390)

By 1979, Ecuador had returned to a system of democratically elected governments. Unfortunately, by the early 1980s, it found itself, along with the rest of Latin America, in a state of economic emergency. The foreign debt that had been accruing since the oil boom of the previous decade brought Ecuador to its knees. As oil prices plummeted and interest rates skyrocketed, Ecuador fell into a black hole of despair. The following data are poignant reminders of just how illusory Ecuador's national euphoria was vis-à-vis its oil boom. During the halcyon days of the early 1970s, Ecuador was selling oil at $35 per barrel; in 1998, prices had fallen to as little as $10 per barrel. In 1970, Ecuador's currency was valued at 25 sucres to 1 U.S. dollar; in 1999, the exchange rate was 18,500 sucres to 1 U.S. dollar. Ecuador's foreign debt grew from $5 billion in 1975 to $12 billion in 1990.

Ecuador's boom-and-bust economy has widened the gap between the rich and the poor. Although Ecuador continues to produce and export cacao, bananas, and oil, the quality of life at the close of the twentieth century has deteriorated significantly. The majority of Ecuadorians now live in cities, and literally millions of people live in squatter settlements, particularly in Guayaquil and Quito. In fact, by 1993, 79 percent of Ecuadorians were officially considered to be living below the poverty level (Grijalva Jiménez 121–122). Moreover, with high inflation and continuous currency devaluations, by the 1990s the government did not have the wherewithal to provide 85 percent of Ecuadorians with basic services such as uninterrupted telephone service, electricity, adequate water, and quality health care (Grijalva Jiménez 120). Although the government's lack of resources and inefficiency have given way to attempts at privatization, that, too, has been stifled by a general lack of foreign investment and capital.

FROM MESTIZO NATION TO *PLURINACIONALIDAD*

Despite Ecuador's dire economic conditions during the last twenty years of the twentieth century, Ecuadorians have not reacted passively, nor have they been waiting for yet another economical "miracle." Indeed, many have been struggling to create new responses to old problems, and it is worth noting that the country's plight has not derailed Ecuadorian democracy, which has been functioning since 1979.

A cursory look at contemporary Ecuador reveals a society that is intensely involved in striking a balance between tradition and change. Urbanization, two-income families, the changing role of women, the growing influence of United States-based Evangelical churches, and the steady increase in computer use are just a few examples of what is happening in Ecuador. There can be no doubt, however, that Ecuador's Indians and Blacks are posing the most significant challenge to the nation's traditions, customs, and long-standing beliefs. What was once considered a mestizo melting pot is now being recast as one nation made up of many nations.

On May 28, 1990, a group of about 100 Indians staged a peaceful takeover of the Santo Domingo Church in Quito. The participants were not an isolated group of malcontents; rather, they represented numerous social activist groups from throughout Ecuador and had a well-planned political agenda. In fact, the takeover was a prelude to a general strike on June 4. On that day, tens of thousands of Indians took to the streets and principal roadways, paralyzing the nation's daily routine. Representatives presented 16 proposals to the government, and for the first time in Ecuador's history, the majority of Ecuadorians understood that the country's Indians could no longer be ignored. The general public finally realized that the issues raised were not just between Indians and landowners; a new political force had emerged, and it was committed to changing the nation (Vallejo 8–10).

On June 6, the protesters left the Santo Domingo Church and a commission was formed to conduct a dialogue between the government and the Indian organizations. Among the 16 proposals drafted by Ecuador's Indians was a declaration that Ecuador constituted an *"estado plurinacional"*; the government was to recognize the Indians' ancestral and territorial rights over the lands they occupied. The Indians defended their right to institute bilingual education in their schools, they argued for greater jurisdiction over legal matters so that their ancestral legal practices would replace standard legal procedures for certain local offenses, they insisted that the government officially recognize the legitimacy of indigenous medicine, and they advocated their taking charge of protecting and developing Ecuador's archaeological sites.

Many Ecuadorians vehemently opposed the Indians' proposals, claiming that Ecuador had only one nationality, and consequently, there could only be one set of laws and standards for the nation's citizens. Despite the continued resistance to the changes proposed by the Indians, a growing number of Ecuadorians have accepted national diversity outside of the traditional mestizo melting pot model. Basically, proponents of Ecuador's *plurinacionalidad* argue that nationality refers to the unity of history, language, and culture of a given social group (Saltos and Vázquez 88). Since Indians, for example, are products of a national experience that has been dramatically different from that of mainstream Ecuadorians, in 1998 the National Assembly formally recommended that Ecuador's constitution openly acknowledge the country's *plurinacionalidad*.

The Indians' insistence on being recognized as distinct nationalities has led to all kinds of distortions. Some of these have been due to a general lack of knowledge about Ecuador's Indians. Basically, the proposals of 1990 were a formal declaration of two realities. First, the nation's indigenous peoples are not homogeneous; there are nine different Indian languages spoken among ten different nationalities. Second, Indians seek a greater participatory role in Ecuadorian society. By defending their rights, they are rejecting long-standing traditions and practices that have treated them like children. Today's Indians, who make up approximately 38 percent of Ecuador's population, have survived and evolved during almost 500 years of conquest and colonialization (Saltos and Vázquez 82). They are well organized, and in light of the inability of governments to solve the nation's problems, they have taken the offensive to ensure that their needs and interests are addressed effectively.

With regard to the public's fears that an official policy of *plurinacionalidad* would lead to political chaos and national disunity, Ecuador has never been characterized by harmony or consensus. Regionalism has long been an obstacle to forging a common national destiny. Moreover, government policies and a rigid class system have, more often than not, excluded the majority of Ecuadorians from meaningful participation in the decision-making process or in the distribution of resources and services. Consequently, Ecuador's nationality debate centers on a restructuring of a very imperfect and unjust system. In defense of the value and validity of the Indians' proposals, one might draw an analogy with what the United States refers to as states' rights. Without proposing the United States as a political model, the point is that local autonomy does not necessarily undermine national unity.

Ecuadorian Blacks are another important piece in the *plurinacional* puzzle. Because most descriptions of Ecuador have emphasized the country's geographical and cultural relation to the Andes, people rarely associate Blacks with Ecuador. Although demographic data vary greatly, most sources indicate that there are between 700,000 and 1,000,000 Ecuadorian Blacks (5–8 percent of the population). Principally located along the Pacific coast in the province of Esmeraldas, Blacks have lived in Ecuador since the mid-sixteenth century.

Ecuadorian Blacks have not maintained or cultivated their African heritage as assiduously as Blacks in Brazil or Haiti, for example. Religious practices and linguistic influences from Africa are uncommon among Ecuador's Afro population. Consequently, few Ecuadorians have been willing to recognize the country's Blacks as forming a separate social group, let alone a distinct nationality. Nevertheless, Afro-Ecuadorian leaders insist that their national experience is unique; they define themselves as a product of slavery and, more important, as a vital expression of the African Diaspora.

Because Ecuador's Blacks have been absent from the national mestizo identity (an identity made up of whites and Indians) that has dominated Ecuadorian politics and culture since before independence, it is no wonder that race and racism have become defining issues for modern-day Blacks. They see their exclusion from long-standing national models of identity as part of the *plurinacional* debate, claiming that the same kinds of appeals to a supposed national unity that have victimized Indians have also denied Blacks their rightful place in society.

The Indian movements that began to gain widespread attention in 1990 have certainly been a source of encouragement for Ecuadorian Blacks to become more active in championing Black awareness. That is not to say, however, that Blacks in previous generations did not speak out against racism or defend issues especially relevant to their communities. From the moment of their arrival in Ecuador, Blacks have rebelled against captivity and oppression, either as runaway slaves or as fugitives living in remote areas called *palenques* (illegal freedom towns). In fact, due to its tropical topography and thick jungle terrain, Esmeraldas has long been a haven for runaways, particularly from Panama and Colombia.

Afro Ecuadorians have a long history of more subtle forms of resistance and rebellion. Many of those who could not flee from their captors and oppressors managed to create and to cultivate alternative lifestyles and forms of expression. The Afro marimba music and the oral poetry called *décimas* are examples of a vibrant Afro culture that has survived centuries of mestizo, or integrationist, policies intended to eliminate all vestiges of a separate Black identity within the nation.

Present-day Blacks have committed themselves to recapturing their past in an effort to promote racial pride. Whereas Afro Ecuadorians in previous generations often tempered references to their racial heritage with emphatic affirmations of their Ecuadorianness—a strategy designed to counter antagonism from mainstream Ecuadorians—today's Blacks do not seek the same kind of acceptance. *Plurinacionalidad* politics is about differences, and in that sense, Afro Ecuadorians have joined the Indian communities in fighting for a restructuring of the Ecuadorian nation.

Today's Indians and Blacks are not simply concerned about local grievances, nor do they see themselves as disconnected from the rest of the nation. More important, they are fighting for greater participation in determining the future of Ecuador. The insistence on territorial rights or on the legitimacy of alternative lifestyles (e.g., medical, legal, and educational practices) is about self-determination, on the one hand, and equal partnership in balancing local and national interests, on the other. In short, Indians and Blacks understand that Ecuador will construct an effective national agenda only when such an agenda is the fruit of the country's complexity and diversity, and a product of a collective effort that is both democratic and *plurinacional.*

PEACE AND THE NEW MILLENNIUM

The debate regarding Ecuador's structure and identity is deeply rooted in that confrontation between Atahualpa and Father Valverde related at the beginning of this chapter. Although the original clash of cultures has evolved through five centuries as a continuous power struggle for absolute domination, one can be cautiously hopeful that today's discussion of *plurinacionalidad* will lead to a more democratic and just resolution. Indeed, as Ecuadorians approach the new millennium, they seem to be committed to revisiting their past and to correcting long-standing misconceptions and ill-conceived practices, be they political, economic, social, or cultural.

The signs that justify such optimism are plentiful. The openness with which Indians and Blacks have defended their claims, the peaceful nature of public protests throughout the country, and the continued respect for the democratic process and free elections indicate a significant change in public attitudes and behavior. These developments are especially noteworthy in that Ecuador finds itself in an economic crisis of unprecedented proportions, a crisis that in the past would have led to military coups and political chaos.

Most important, however, is the peace agreement signed by Ecuador and Peru on October 26, 1998, in Brasilia, Brazil. After more than 100 years of hostilities over border disputes and claims of territorial sovereignty, Ecuador's government finally agreed to put to rest a prolonged conflict that has drained untold resources and disrupted far too many projects that were created to address society's most pressing needs. In short, Ecuador has accepted its borders as defined by the 1942 Protocolo de Río de Janeiro, an accord that in the past had been considered high treason.

To be sure, Ecuadorians will struggle with ghosts of times past, and they will occasionally succumb to internal and external forces that will frustrate their attempts to create new solutions to old problems. Be that as it may, the signing of the 1998 peace accord and the ongoing debate over *plurinacionalidad* suggest the dawning of a new age in Ecuadorian history. Upon assuming the presidency on August 10, 1998, Jamil Mahuad quoted from Ecclesiastes 3:1–2 in his inaugural address:

> For everything there is a season,
> and a time for every matter under heaven:
> a time to be born, and a time to die; . . .

At the peace accord signing ceremony, President Mahuad again referred to Ecclesiastes:

> And today we are born and do not die; we heal
> and do not kill; . . . we love and
> do not hate because we are building peace
> instead of making war.

It would appear that President Mahaud's inaugural message and the peace treaty mark yet another defining moment in Ecuadorian history. In 1895, the Liberal Revolution ushered new expectations and greater tolerance for a more open society. Despite its shortcomings and failures, that revolution did propel Ecuador into modernity. One can only hope that President Mahuad's message is a testimony of Ecuador's newborn courage and resolve to confront the challenges of underdevelopment with compassion, understanding, and creative vision.

REFERENCES

Anderson, Benedict. *Imagined Communities: Reflections on the Origin and Spread of Nationalism.* Rev. ed. London: Verso, 1991.

Ayala Mora, Enrique. *Resumen de historia del Ecuador.* Quito: Corporación Editora Nacional, 1997.

Benites Vinueza, Leopoldo. *Ecuador: Drama y paradoja.* Quito: Banco Central del Ecuador y Corporación Editora Nacional, 1986.

Carrión, Benjamín. *Cartas al Ecuador.* Quito: Banco Central del Ecuador, 1988.

Chaves, Fernando. *El hombre ecuatoriano y su cultura.* Quito: Banco Central del Ecuador, 1990.

Grijalva Jiménez, Agustín, ed. *Datos básicos de la realidad nacional.* Quito: Corporación Editora Nacional, 1996.

Lara, Jorge Salvador. *Breve historia contemporánea del Ecuador.* 2nd ed. Mexico City: Fondo de Cultura Económica, 1995.

Mahuad, Jamil. "Mahuad: Ejerzamos la paz de Forma permanente." *El Universo* (October 27, 1998), 1.

Martz, John. *Politics and Petroleum in Ecuador.* New Brunswick, NJ: Transaction Books, 1987.

Saltos G., Napoleón, and Lola Vázquez, eds. *Ecuador: Su realidad.* 5th ed. Quito: Fundación "José Peralta," 1997.

Vallejo, Raúl. *Crónica mestiza del Nuevo Pachakutik.* Working Paper no. 2. College Park: University of Maryland, 1996.

2

Religion

Religion is a controversial topic in Ecuador's history. At times, it has served to nurture the spiritual and cultural well-being of the country. At other times, however, it has been a means to seize power and privilege in a highly stratified society.

Like most Latin American countries, Ecuador is basically Catholic. Of the 5 to 10 percent of the population not within the Catholic Church, most belong to a Protestant church. Although there are Ecuadorians who profess other faiths (e.g., Jews and Muslims), they are small in number and, historically, too peripheral for consideration here.

Briefly, Ecuador's Catholic Church has 4 archdioceses, 10 dioceses, some 140 religious orders, approximately 1,000 parishes, 4 universities, 2 radio stations, and 2 television stations (Saltos and Vázquez 252). Most of Ecuador's Protestant churches came to the country from the United States. The Methodist, Anglican, Lutheran, Baptist, and Presbyterian churches have not had much of a presence in the country; during the last half of the twentieth century, it is the Evangelical and Pentecostal churches that have had an increasingly significant impact on Ecuadorian religion and cultural mores. There are about 260 Evangelical denominations in Ecuador (Grijalva Jiménez 67–68), and by 1986 there were 250,000 practicing worshipers (Goffin xx), most of whom were members of the rural and urban poor.

Clearly, then, Catholic priests and Protestant missionaries dominate Ecuador's religious landscape. Together, they form a large cadre of Christian soldiers committed to saving souls and to winning converts to their respective churches. Notwithstanding their faith in Jesus Christ, they have little in

common. In fact, during much of the twentieth century, Catholics and Protestants have been staunch rivals, each suspicious and contemptuous of the
other.

The Catholic priests arrived in Ecuador in the early sixteenth century with
the Spanish conquerors; the Protestant missionaries began to make their
presence felt at the end of the nineteenth century, the period of the beginnings of Ecuadorian liberalism and the emergence of U.S. imperialism. In
each case, because the historical circumstances tended to consolidate spiritual
and political objectives, the people were too often pawns in a religious battle
designed to serve foreign interests more than their own. On the one hand,
Indian heathens would be saved from their pagan ways and integrated into
the Spanish Empire; on the other hand, the poor and destitute would find
financial and technical support for their material needs while following a
North American path to salvation. Despite the many promised benefits
throughout the centuries, dependence would frequently be a costly price to
pay for religious conversion.

CATHOLICISM: FROM CONQUEST TO LIBERALISM

The confrontation between Atahualpa and Father Vicente de Valverde
described in the first chapter of this book clearly illustrates the role Catholicism would play in Ecuador prior to the last half of the twentieth century.
The Catholic Church demanded obedience and blind faith from the people.
In many ways, the massive churches and cathedrals that dominate the center
of each city evoke the church's power and authority. Moreover, the material
wealth and artistic splendor of such baroque churches as Quito's La Compañía de Jesús (the Company of Jesus) stand in marked contrast to the population's humble living conditions. As tourists marvel at the Compañía's
beauty, the beggars of all ages who crowd its doorway are a sore reminder of
Father Valverde's legacy of contradiction and paradox.

The human costs that made possible such awe-inspiring structures must
not be forgotten. In the name of salvation, the Spanish Crown and Catholic
Church established the *encomienda* system, under which Indians gave their
free labor for protection and Christian guidance. As the sixteenth-century
priest Bartolomé de Las Casas proclaimed in the Caribbean, such a system
was abusive and oppressive throughout the Americas. Ecuador was no exception. At the expense of the Indians, the Spanish Crown, its allied landowners,
and the church amassed fortunes in gold and minerals.

Although the church became one of Ecuador's principal landowners, not
all priests were motivated by personal wealth and riches. Dominicans, Fran-

Church domes at the center of colonial Cuenca. Courtesy of James Minton.

ciscans, Jesuits, and Augustinians brought seeds and tools. Many were active in education, founding schools and universities (Hurtado 211). "In 1552, two Flemish friars, Jodoko [sic] Ricke and Pedro Gosseal, founded the first New World school of arts and crafts. These craftsmen taught native artisans their skills" (Goffin 8). By the late sixteenth and early seventeenth centuries, Quito had become known as the city of convents, "and from there the newly arrived clergy set out through the Sierra and into the Oriente to evangelize indigenous people" (Goffin 3).

The initial attempts to evangelize were not without difficulties and extreme sacrifice. Catholic missionaries had to communicate complex religious concepts and beliefs in a language that did not have a written alphabet. Furthermore, Ecuador's Indians had their own complex set of religious beliefs and practices that would not merely disappear with the Spanish conquest. In fact, one of the country's unique cultural features is its profoundly syncretic brand of Catholicism that combines many pre-Columbian and European icons, ceremonies, and rituals.

For successful religious conversion, the clergy went to great lengths to accommodate Indian traditions. Because Indians were accustomed to elaborate ceremonies, for example, the missionaries astutely incorporated processions, solemn masses, and impressive fiestas into the Catholic Church's practices. Similarly, churches and sanctuaries were built in places that Indians had considered sacred, thus assuring a continuity between conquest and colonization.

Although the clergy had designed strategies to create a smooth transition from so-called paganism to Catholicism, they inadvertently created conditions that would guarantee the survival of many important aspects of the Indians' traditional religious beliefs. A case in point is the sacred statues and relics that not only represent the church's official pantheon of saints but also evoke the pre-Columbian gods who shared similar powers. From the point of view of the Indians, whose languages and beliefs were never fully understood by most Spanish and other European missionaries, however, the apparent process of mutual adaptation and assimilation frequently constituted a subtle form of cultural resistance. In fact, many have argued that the survival of indigenous religious practices demonstrates that the Conquest was not as definitive as reported.

Notwithstanding the politics inherent in the interactions between the Catholic Church and the indigenous communities, the Ecuadorian experience is a vivid reminder that one can find cultural syncretism throughout Latin America. This is especially true in regions where large Indian and African populations have been integrated into societies that were colonized by such European powers as Spain, France, and Portugal. The dynamic contact between the different cultures in Ecuadorian Catholicism demonstrates the degree to which the Indians and Blacks were active participants in the creation and development of the New World.

Unfortunately, and paradoxically, not everyone has recognized or welcomed such hybridity. For some, acceptance of Indians and Blacks as protagonists in Ecuadorian (and Latin American) cultural history would be tantamount to destroying traditional class, racial, and ethnic distinctions of privilege and power. For others, who are unfamiliar with indigenous traditions and culture, the coexistence of religious beliefs and practices has frequently been elusive and difficult to identify. In fact, outside of Ecuador's Indian and Afro communities, Catholicism's prevailing features are Western and, more specifically, Hispanic.

It is no wonder that the Catholic Church's hierarchy and Ecuador's ruling elites have traditionally preferred to identify the church with its European heritage, particularly when celebrating its past heroes and leaders. One could argue that such a skewed view springs from the "civilization and barbarianism" conflict that has shaped so much of Ecuador's official history. Unfortunately, the church's reluctance or unwillingness to embrace openly and broadly the creativity and dynamic nature of its non-European past (and present) has relegated the majority of the church's followers to a position of subservience and inferiority. Moreover, such stratification among its members has deprived the church of invaluable human resources that will be essential if it is to be a guiding force in a society struggling to come to terms with its multicultural and plurinational heritage.

CHURCH HEROES AND NATIONAL PATRIMONY

Despite the Catholic Church's questionable politics vis-à-vis Ecuador's masses prior to the last half of the twentieth century, the church has produced many individuals who have contributed significantly to Ecuador's national patrimony. Beginning in the sixteenth century, the church was a dynamic source of religious and civic role models. Church officials and priests have greatly influenced Ecuadorian music, art, architecture, history, and literature. In the early years, these leaders were Europeans. In time, however, the church's gallery of heroes became Ecuadorian. In their respective ways, Santa Mariana de Jesús, Gabriel García Moreno, and Father Federico González Suárez have come to epitomize the traditional Catholic Church in Ecuador.

Santa Mariana de Jesús

Among Ecuador's many local patron saints, Mariana de Jesús occupies a special place. Born in 1618 to a wealthy Quito family, she was a paragon of self-sacrifice and virtue. Her life was one of prayer, catechism, and aid to the needy. In addition to her customary fasting and acts of penitence, Mariana was famous for her unfailing obedience to her spiritual mentor, the missionary Alonso de Rojas. In 1645, Mariana de Jesús died three days after publicly offering her life for the health and safety of Quito, a city that was buffeted by earthquakes and pestilence. Public reaction at her funeral signaled the beginnings of an effort to canonize Mariana. In 1850, Pope Pius IX beatified her; in 1946, Ecuador's National Assembly formally recognized her as a national heroine (*heroína nacional*); in 1950, Pope Pius XII canonized her; and finally, during his 1985 visit to Ecuador, Pope John Paul II officially named Mariana de Jesús "Saint Mariana of Quito" (Lara 223).

Gabriel García Moreno

Gabriel García Moreno, twice Ecuador's president (1861–1865, 1869–1875), is another central character in the nation's relationship with the Catholic Church. During his second presidency, he dedicated the country to the

Sacred Heart of Jesus as a supreme sign of devotion. Although it is difficult to separate García Moreno's political motives from his religious ones, it is clear that he saw Ecuador as a theocratic state. For him, the church and the government were partners; an 1863 concordat gave the Vatican "undisputed control of all education, freedom to publish papal bulls without state interference, and restoration of ecclesiastical courts" (Herring 580). In 1861 Congress had ratified a new constitution that made Catholicism Ecuador's only legal religion. In 1869, García Moreno was instrumental in the writing of yet another constitution; this time citizenship was granted only to practicing Catholics.

García Moreno's government was rife with conflict, and his religious fanaticism was the source of most of the period's tensions. In the name of Christian morality, García Moreno was relentless in persecuting his rivals. It is no wonder that Benjamín Carrión titled his 1959 biography of García Moreno *Santo del Patíbulo* (Saint of the Gallows).

Father Federico González Suárez

The life and works of Father Federico González Suárez (1844–1917) exemplify the close relationship between the religious and the secular in Ecuadorian history. From his pulpit as bishop of Ibarra (1894) and archbishop of Quito (1906), González Suárez dominated Ecuador's social, political, and cultural life of the late nineteenth and early twentieth centuries. He was a historian, literary critic, religious scholar, and archaeologist. In 1894, he was a national senator. His power and authority were so absolute that the enactment of government policies often depended upon his favorable opinion and ultimate approval (Barrera 31).

With his monumental seven-volume *Historia general de la República del Ecuador* (General History of Ecuador) that he began publishing in 1890, González Suárez influenced the way future generations would write history. Unlike his predecessors, who used history to prove and justify what they already believed, he was assiduous in gathering the facts that would be the basis for his conclusions about Ecuador's colonial history. Especially noteworthy in the *Historia general* was his documentation of the sinful and intemperate ways of many Catholic priests and missionaries in previous centuries. Although his findings were initially criticized and condemned by Ecuador's Catholics, his honesty and commitment to the truth were ultimately endorsed by the Vatican (Barrera 31).

Despite his willingness to criticize the church and its clergy openly, González Suárez was vehement and tireless in his opposition to Eloy Alfaro and the liberals' anticlericalism that began in earnest in 1895. González Suárez understood that Catholicism was under attack and that religion as a faith and as an institution would never be quite the same in Ecuador. Indeed, his death in 1917 marked the end of an era for the Catholic Church in Ecuador. No other church official would ever wield the kind of power or influence that characterized González Suárez and some of his predecessors.

PROTESTANTISM AND SOCIAL CHANGE

As Alfaro and his liberal followers displaced Ecuador's traditional conservative oligarchy with the 1895 Revolution, the Catholic Church suffered significant losses of wealth and power. Unlike the García Moreno regime, which considered the church to be a ruling partner, Alfaro's government insisted on the separation of powers and the overarching authority of a secular state. New laws that guaranteed civil marriage, divorce, and public education loosened the church's hold over society; nationalization of many of the church's landholdings weakened its financial base.

Naturally, the church and its conservative supporters organized to oppose Alfaro's policies. In light of the political conflicts and religious tensions caused by the break between the church and the state, Alfaro was only too eager to welcome Protestant missions to Ecuador. In fact,

the Liberals in Ecuador and the North American Protestants entered into a symbiotic relationship. The Liberals used the Protestants to weaken the Conservatives' hold on power, while the Protestants utilized the Liberals to gain a foothold from which to build their movement. (Goffin 33)

During the first decades after their official arrival in Ecuador, Protestant missionaries met with considerable resistance and opposition from the Catholic Church and its supporters. Protestants were denounced as children of Satan, and Ecuadorians were warned that associating with the intruders would lead to eternal damnation. Notwithstanding the church's aggressive attacks and its presence for nearly 500 years in Ecuador, the Protestant missionaries were steadfast in their commitment to establishing themselves among Ecuadorians. Because such early groups as the Gospel Missionary Union and the Christian and Missionary Alliance were products of U.S. fundamentalism, they succeeded in creating a network of U.S. supporters who were interested in sponsoring and financing their church-related projects.

In comparison with the Catholic Church and its clergy, the Protestant missionaries brought to Ecuador a strikingly different modus operandi. Instead of opulence, magnificent churches, and unquestioned power, Protestant leaders consciously forged an image of humility and camaraderie. The allure of their religious message had much to do with the community development projects they carried out for the poor; running water, latrines, irrigation ditches, and health-care facilities seemed to confirm the righteousness of their work and intentions.

The growth of the Protestant communities has been slow in Ecuador during the twentieth century. In fact, they constituted less than 3 percent of the population in 1985. Based on some projections, however, by 2010, Protestants conceivably could comprise as much as 15.7 percent of the population (Stoll 337).

Regardless of their numbers, it is clear that Protestants have deeply affected the way many Ecuadorians view religion and religious institutions, especially since the 1960s. The Catholic Church has modified its approach to teaching the Gospel and to promoting community relations. In contrast with its past insistence on strict obedience and absolute authority, the Ecuadorian Bishops' Conference of 1979 issued eight pastoral goals: evangelization, defense of the poor, development of Christian Base Communities, lay participation, reexamination of popular religious practices, support for local churches, promotion of a missionary spirit, and encouragement of vocations (Goffin 112).

HCJB: The Voice of the Andes

After three decades of gradually settling into Ecuador, in 1931, Protestants initiated a project that would revolutionize religion and religious worship for years to come. The World Radio Missionary Fellowship and the Christian and Missionary Alliance founded the Voice of the Andes, also known as HCJB (Heralding Christ Jesus' Blessings), the first Evangelical radio station to operate outside the United States (Goffin 41). The radio station's managers loaned people radio receivers so they could listen to the Gospel in groups in the most remote regions of the country. No longer limited to a fixed locale or by an inadequate number of ministers, the Protestant leadership utilized the airwaves to create a ubiquitous and mobile church.

In 1941, the Christian and Missionary Alliance extended its presence by deciding to broadcast programs and religious services in the Quechua language. Quechua transmission "grew to provide more than a hundred hours a week in the language and reached an audience that may have exceeded

14 million listeners in Southern Colombia, Ecuador, Peru, Bolivia, and Northern Argentina" (Goffin 43). By the late 1980s, the Voice of the Andes could be heard in 11 languages.

HCJB's revolutionary use of technology moved into television, and it aired the first television program ever produced in Ecuador in 1960. In fact, "The Window of the Andes" was the first missionary television station in the world (Goffin 43). However, due to a lack of staff and facilities, and numerous laws that limited its operations, HCJB eventually was forced to sell its television broadcasting rights to commercial investors. By later producing and distributing religious videos as part of its evangelical mission, HCJB demonstrated once again an ability to anticipate technological and market-driven opportunities for the delivery of its religious message.

HCJB's widespread exposure in Ecuador and elsewhere produced a huge financial base of support, especially from U.S. contributors. Financial resources made it possible for HCJB to be much more than a radio or television station. By 1946, it had become involved in health care, and by 1958, it had built two hospitals in Ecuador. Ecuadorian governments were only too happy for HCJB and other Evangelical organizations to provide the poor with such needed services. Unfortunately, as many critics often claimed, HCJB had become a persuasive political force that was supposedly disruptive, intrusive, and motivated by principles that had little to do with Ecuadorian values and traditions, or even with the dissemination of the Gospel.

Summer Institute of Linguistics

Controversy also surrounded the work of the Summer Institute of Linguistics (SIL), another fundamentalist Protestant group based in the United States. The Summer Institute of Linguistics proposed to translate the Bible into all of the world's languages. Although it did not officially begin its work in Ecuador until 1952, it had collaborated with HCJB as early as 1946. Among its guiding principles was the belief that all groups were worthy of linguistic study, and that no language was too difficult to translate. SIL was committed to taking the Bible to the most remote areas of the world, where it would teach the Gospel in the native language.

Despite its linguistic and research agenda, in 1953, SIL received from the Ecuadorian government "tax-exempt status reserved for religious organizations that worked in the Oriente" (Goffin 57). In 1956, five of its missionaries were brutally killed by a group of Huaorani Indians, and years later, SIL was accused of secretly collaborating with foreign oil companies that wanted the Huaorani to abandon their lands, which were rich in oil reserves. Criticism of SIL became so intense by 1981 that President Jaime Roldós expelled the group from Ecuador that year.

World Vision

In the 1980s, World Vision was yet another fundamentalist organization that provoked controversy and conflict. Although it claimed to work for the well-being of Ecuador's indigenous communities, its critics insist that World Vision "was a perfect example of a wealthy North American agency trying to buy the loyalty of the poor" (Stoll 267). Moreover, "Ecuadorians began to suspect that World Vision's humanitarian rhetoric concealed a plan to divide peasant communities and break up their political organizations" (Stoll 268).

As had been the case with HCJB and SIL, World Vision controlled sufficient resources to position itself as an attractive alternative to most religious and secular national organizations that were unable to meet the urgent needs of Ecuador's poor. The seemingly unlimited wealth of World Vision (and of other Protestant organizations in Ecuador), coupled with the financial crises characteristic of Ecuador's governments, could only lead to a dangerous imbalance of power. As people lost confidence in their government and social institutions to provide basic services (e.g., running water, electricity, telephone service, and quality schools), World Vision threatened to wrest away the people's loyalty and allegiance.

Many Ecuadorians believe World Vision has created among its beneficiaries a passive mentality conditioned to seek foreign assistance instead of real social change. Specifically, World Vision has been "likened to Santa Claus's bringing gifts in return for passivity and a belief in the New Testament. World Vision was also compared to the SIL and accused of the cultural and physical destruction of indigenous people" (Goffin 79).

Readers from the United States may find it difficult to understand many of the reasons behind the vehement protests lodged against such organizations as World Vision. There certainly continues to be an urgent need for improved social and medical services. Unfortunately, charity does not usually create conditions for self-sufficiency. Moreover, since the 1950s, Evangelical churches and missionaries have frequently been linked to right-wing politicians and political parties that have not sought to change the prevailing social, economic, and political structures of their respective countries. Neoliberalism, globalization, and an emphasis on individualism and material wealth have frequently been an intrinsic part of evangelism in Ecuador and other developing nations. It is no wonder that many Ecuadorians have denounced Protestant churches as being conduits for U.S. cultural imperialism.

THE RESURGENCE OF THE CATHOLIC CHURCH

The Catholic Church in Ecuador and throughout Latin America underwent a major revision beginning in the 1960s. Liberation theology—a theology committed to social justice and political activism—became the church's predominant defining principle. Not only did liberation theology constitute a significant departure from the church's traditional role in society, but it was also a uniquely Latin American response to the changing times that would distinguish the church from its North American-based Protestant rivals.

Unlike the Evangelical groups that combined salvation and relief work without addressing the multiple causes of poverty and injustice, Latin America's new wave of Catholics defined salvation in terms of social justice. With regard to the church's long-standing belief that salvation would be given in an afterlife, and that it was a purely personal experience dependent upon the grace of God, liberation theologists taught not only that the Kingdom of God was accessible on Earth, but also that it was earned by fighting for justice in this life. In effect, resignation and acceptance of one's fate had been replaced by a socially committed mentality that considered injustice to be man's only real sin (Silva Gotay 131).

Because liberation theology influenced the Catholic Church and its followers in multiple ways, it would be a mistake to look for a monolithic or universal response to the general call for justice and salvation. While the Colombian priest Camilo Torres, for example, concluded that armed struggle was the only means of creating the Kingdom of God on Earth, others preferred strategies of nonviolence. Unfortunately, nonviolent activism for social change was frequently met by persecution, torture, and even death. That ugly reality was tragically exemplified by El Salvador's Archbishop Oscar Romero, who was murdered while celebrating mass in 1980.

Archbishop Leonidas Proaño, Ecuador's "Bishop of the Andes"

Archbishop Leonidas Proaño (1910–1988) was Ecuador's leading advocate of liberation theology. He carried out his pastoral work in Chimborazo province, which is high in the Andes and home to the country's largest Indian population. Archbishop Proaño struggled incessantly for health care, proper working conditions, land reform, and quality education for Ecuador's Indians. In 1986, he was nominated for the Nobel Peace Prize.

Born and raised in the Sierra, Proaño had a clear understanding of the Indians' ways and the historical circumstances that formed their sense of personal and collective identity. In his opinion, that understanding qualified him as a credible and effective advocate for his people and separated him from most North American Protestant missionaries (Goffin 115). "In Chimborazo, Proaño organized literacy campaigns by radio for the indigenous population, established peasant leader hostels and schools, vetoed the construction of an elaborate cathedral, stripped territorial holdings from the church in his jurisdiction, and adopted a life-style of 'total evangelical poverty' " (Goffin 115–116).

Although his detractors often accused him of being a Marxist, Proaño actually

> feared violent revolution, in particular the number of Indians he knew would be killed making one. Preaching against ideological borrowing from Marxism, he favored what he called an authentically Christian theology of liberation. Instead of socialism, he preferred to speak of a "communitarian option," based on indigenous campesino tradition, which would somehow save Latin America from the destruction and strife of capitalism. (Stoll 276)

While Ecuador was still under a military dictatorship in 1976, Proaño was involved in an incident that clearly illustrated the degree to which he was feared for his revolutionary message of peace and social justice. With the approval of the Vatican and Ecuador's church leadership, Proaño organized an international meeting in Chimborazo to discuss his pastoral program. Seventeen archbishops from various Latin American countries and numerous leading theologians attended the conference. Despite the participants' credentials and the openness of the meeting's agenda, the national police, armed with machine guns, arrested Proaño and his guests because the government had accused them of conspiring to overthrow it (Goffin 116).

According to some Ecuadorians, the government's actions were part of a larger plan among various military dictatorships to undermine Latin America's radicalized church. Be that as it may, Proaño devoted his efforts to making religion relevant to the daily lives of his people. "He believed in the nobility of mankind and taught that peace could not coexist with oppression, injustice, and torture, all of which he knew were taking place in Ecuador and elsewhere in the Americas" (Goffin 117).

Since his death in 1988, many members of the church have continued to develop Archbishop Proaño's progressive teachings and social projects. Of special importance is the growing ecumenical movement that came of age in 1978 when Catholic and Protestant liberation theologians joined forces with labor organizations to create the Ecumenical Human Rights Commission of Ecuador. Under the leadership of Elsie Monge, an Ecuadorian Maryknoll sister, the Commission publicly denounced human rights violations that had occurred in Ecuador. Basically, the Commission

> believed it had a duty to work with any and all organizations that promoted basic human rights and attempted to satisfy the needs of poor people everywhere. It was mindful of the fact that there were vast differences between the North American fundamentalist Protestants and the more ecumenical national and Latin American churches. (Goffin 122)

CONCLUSION

Religion has always been a powerful force in Ecuador. During pre-Columbian times, Indians worshiped the sun and organized their lives around their religious beliefs and rituals. After the Conquest, Catholicism was at the core of a society governed by both the church and the state. Although Protestant groups eventually challenged the Catholic Church's preeminence in Ecuador, the centrality of religion in people's lives has never been brought into question.

The steady growth of Protestantism and the emergence of liberation theology clearly demonstrate the vital role religion continues to play in Ecuador. During the past 50 years in Ecuador and in the rest of Latin America, traditional hierarchical structures in the Catholic Church have been challenged, and some have been broken; similarly, much controversy and debate have surrounded the social and political agenda that characterizes the region's North American–based Protestant churches. Notwithstanding the conflicts at the institutional level of the different churches, the people have continued to appropriate those religious forms and practices that best meet their needs.

Through the centuries, Catholic and Protestant churches have too often functioned as institutional elites whose evangelization projects have ignored the ability of people to take charge of their own lives. Nevertheless, whether one refers to religious syncretism or to each church's growing commitment to greater lay participation in church affairs, the people have always been actively engaged in defining their spiritual lives. That vitality, coupled with myriad progressive churches and church activists devoted to human rights and social justice, signals that religion continues to be alive and well in Ecuador.

REFERENCES

Barrera, Isaac. *Diccionario de la literatura latinoamericana: Ecuador.* Washington, DC: Unión Panamericana, 1962.

Goffin, Alvin M. *The Rise of Protestant Evangelism in Ecuador, 1895–1990.* Gainesville: University Press of Florida, 1994.

Grijalva Jiménez, Agustín, ed. *Datas básicos de la realidad nacional.* Quito: Corporación Editora Nacional, 1996.

Herring, Hubert. *A History of Latin America.* 3rd. ed. New York: Alfred A. Knopf, 1968.

Hurtado, Oswaldo. *Dos mundos superpuestos (Ensayo de diagnósitico de la realidad Ecuatoriana).* Quito: INEDES, 1969.

Lara, Jorge Salvador. *Breve historia contemporánea del Ecuador.* Mexico City: Fondo de Cultura Económica, 1995.

Proaño, Leonidas. "La iglesia y los sectores populares 1830–1980." In *Politica y Sociedad. Ecuador: 1830–1980.* Ed. Enrique Ayala Mora. Quito: Corporación Editora Nacional, 1980.

Rodríguez Castelo, Hernán, ed. *Letras de la Audiencia de Quito: Período Jesuítico.* Caracas: Biblioteca Ayacucho, 1984.

Saltos G., Napoleón, and Lola Vázquez, eds. *Ecuador: Su realidad.* 5th ed. Quito: Fundación "José Peralta," 1997.

Silva Gotay, Samuel. "El pensamiento religioso." In *América Latina en Sus Ideas.* Ed. Leopoldo Zea. Mexico City: Siglo Veintiuno Editores, 1986. 118–154.

Stoll, David. *Is Latin America Turning Protestant? The Politics of Evangelical Growth.* Berkeley: University of California Press, 1990.

3

Social Customs

For some Ecuadorians, a typical day might include checking e-mail, going to a shopping mall, eating a Whopper at Burger King, watching an NBA basketball game on ESPN, and renting one of Hollywood's latest box office hits at Blockbuster. One might be tempted to conclude that globalization has created a common culture among the world's diverse nations, especially in the Americas. As for the tourists who casually wander into one of Ecuador's spacious malls and feel at home, they would do well to keep in mind that appearances are often deceiving. While it is true that most Ecuadorians enthusiastically embrace many features of the American way of life, they are not clones who simply mirror their influential northern neighbors. Notwithstanding their political and economic dependence on the United States, Ecuadorians have been steadfast in cultivating and defending their Ecuadorianness. The following discussion about the country's social customs will highlight some of the principal cultural practices that give Ecuador its uniqueness. (Because of the vastness of the topic, particular attention will be given to those customs most readily found in Ecuador's principal cities.)

It is important to remember that the notion of Ecuadorianness should not suggest either unchanging characteristics or cultural homogeneity. Ecuadorians are always evolving, and they do not constitute a one-dimensional or monolithic society. Geographic, class, ethnic, and generational differences have given rise to customs that one would not necessarily categorize as being national or common to all Ecuadorians. Similarly, Ecuador's cultural practices do not exist in a vacuum, and thus one would be hard pressed to find a custom that belongs only to Ecuadorians.

The reference to a shopping mall is a useful starting point for a discussion about social customs. Just as in the United States, shopping malls in Ecuador have become favorite climate-controlled meeting places that offer myriad activities. Shops, food courts, and movie theaters spill over with enthusiastic patrons of all ages. Posters of Michael Jordan abound; Levis, pizza, rap, computers, automatic teller machines, and credit cards are everywhere—yet this is not the United States!

Shopping malls are frequented by middle-class and upper-middle-class Ecuadorians; they are exclusive to a small segment of society, and as such, they represent a break with the traditional public plaza and open markets that are the gathering places of the country's masses. This separation is largely due to economics and traditional social class distinctions. Few Ecuadorians have the wherewithal to take part in the shopping mall culture. Furthermore, the demographics of shopping malls are a reminder of just how stratified Ecuadorian society is. While the well-to-do continue to isolate themselves behind the walls of their elegant country clubs and posh social clubs, the middle and upper-middle classes have appropriated the shopping malls as their exclusive space. Naturally, such exclusivity presupposes a social status that must be protected, cultivated, and flaunted. A visit to the mall requires the right attire, and the highly informal dress so common in the United States would not be appropriate. After all, clothes symbolize a kind of material elegance that publicly confirms each person's station in life.

Class consciousness permeates every facet of life in Ecuador. Surnames, club memberships, enrollment at certain schools, and influential business connections are some of the means Ecuadorians employ to distinguish the elite (or aspiring elite) from the country's "rabble." The pyramid structure that governs standard relationships among the social classes in Ecuador comes in no small measure from the country's Hispanic heritage, on the one hand, and from a cultural legacy deeply rooted in the image of "civilization and barbarianism," on the other. Besides the many injustices that such hierarchial relations have created through the centuries in Ecuador's larger economic and political arenas, they have had a profound effect on the way many people deal with others on a daily basis.

Bureaucrats, public servants, and even store clerks are infamous for their lack of courtesy and disdainful attitude to strangers and the public in general. Ecuadorians simply do not recognize that "the customer is always right." At some fundamental level, such relations are defined by an underlying tension created by the apparent need to establish one's authority and control. Obtaining a permit or an official document frequently becomes a nightmare of futility and frustration in Ecuador. *Póngase en fila* (stand on line), *vuelva mañana* (come back tomorrow), *no hay cómo* (it cannot be done), *no se atiende hoy* (no service today), and the curt *no tenemos* (we don't have any) are just a few of the stock expressions used to keep people in their place.

However, the harsh and cold demeanor so characteristic of public dealings quickly becomes cordial and effusive when Ecuadorians recognize a face or a name. *Personalismo* (personal influence), *palanca* (the right contacts), and *compadrazgo* (the relationship between parents and godparents) are key factors that enable Ecuadorians to navigate successfully in a system that puts such a premium on social status and social connections. At every step of the way, *personal* contacts and influence determine who stands on line and who obtains the required permits.

THE EXTENDED FAMILY

Traditionally, Ecuadorian households commonly included several generations of a family under one roof. Although many Ecuadorians have become more independent and geographically mobile than in the past, modern families continue to see themselves as being close-knit and broadly inclusive. Indeed, the extended family still occupies a central place in the lives of most Ecuadorians. The intricate web of relatives is frequently far-reaching so that members have greater access to all kinds of opportunities in society. The personal connections are a guarantee that, when necessary, one will find the appropriate person with leverage or pull (*palanca*).

The *Compadrazgo* System and Family Relations

Compadrazgo has long been a key component in the extended family. Deeply rooted in the Catholic Church, people utilize the baptism and First Communion of their children to broaden their sphere of influence and mutual cooperation. The selection of a child's godparents is done carefully and thoughtfully. *Compadrazgo* frequently implies a relationship of reciprocity: the less fortunate often turn to their superiors to ensure that their children will always have protection, and the godparents and godchildren know that they can always count on assistance and support from their baptismal family.

Parents and godparents refer to themselves as *compadres*, and that relationship is taken very seriously. The *compadres* are not necessarily from different social classes. The *compadrazgo* system works the same way among social equals as it does for those who are not of the same social rank: no sacrifice is too great for any member of the extended family.

The personal relationships between *compadres* and between godparents and godchildren, fill a social void that has been created by institutions unable or unwilling to provide people with needed services. In response to the system's inefficiency and indifference, the majority of Ecuadorians have learned how to work around it rather than through it. In effect, the contacts made within the *compadrazgo* culture guarantee personal attention to one's needs.

PEOPLE ENJOYING PEOPLE

As one might expect in a society where so much emphasis is placed on personal contacts, Ecuadorians do not generally value private space or private time as much as people from the United States do. In Ecuador people define themselves in terms of friends and the extended family; regardless of their work schedules and personal commitments, Ecuadorians find time to cultivate their relationships. Indeed, people in Ecuador genuinely enjoy each other.

Private and Public Fiestas

The fiesta is at the core of social life in Ecuador. Birthdays, graduations, baptisms, anniversaries, and weddings are just a few of the many occasions that Ecuadorians celebrate. Typically, fiestas are given at private homes and feature abundant food, drink, and music. Unlike the dinner party or social gathering in the United States, Ecuadorian fiestas begin late, frequently last until dawn, and are extremely loud. Guests rarely arrive before 10 P.M.; at about 2 A.M., after several hours of socializing and dancing, the hosts usually serve a large meal specially prepared for the fiesta. When the meal is finished, the music again begins to blare; guests frequently dance until breakfast, when everyone caps off the long night with ceviche, a bowl of uncooked, marinated fish or shrimp.

It is not unusual for parties to include live music. Small combos or a singer with an electric organ are quite common. There are no laws to control the noise level from the fiesta. In Ecuador, the neighbors are expected to respect the revelers and their right to celebrate.

One of the most popular reasons for a fiesta is the *quinceañera* birthday party. Somewhat similar to the sweet sixteen celebration in the United States, the *quinceañera* is a girl who turns fifteen and whose parents (or perhaps her godparents) host a coming-of-age party for friends and relatives. Depending upon the family's resources, the fiesta is either at home or at a social club. Because it is customary for the *quinceañera* to wear a pink dress, Ecuadorians frequently describe the celebration as a *fiesta rosada* (a pink party).

Many parents announce the *quinceañera* party in the local newspaper and include a recent photograph of the girl. The celebration tends to be quite formal. Guests often dress elegantly, and someone special is chosen to offer a toast in honor of the *quinceañera*. This particular birthday party is not limited to the girl's friends; guests of all ages join together and literally dance the night away.

Fiestas are not limited to private functions. Public celebrations are common in Ecuador. Cities and small towns commemorate independence and founder's day, or they honor a local patron saint with parades, concerts, block parties, and official visits from political dignitaries. Street vendors are found everywhere, particularly those who hawk food and beverages. The fiesta means that the daily routine stops: schools and business close; public parks, plazas, restaurants, open-air markets, and dance clubs overflow with people.

Some of the fiestas attract large numbers of tourists. For example, Guayaquil's Independence Day is October 9, Cuenca's is November 3, and Quito celebrates Founder's Day on December 6. Musical groups and marching bands from other cities and regions commonly participate in the festivities as a gesture of respect and solidarity between neighbors. Long into the night one can hear the jubilant shouts of *Viva Guayaquil! Viva Cuenca! Viva Quito!*

Although Ecuador does not celebrate Carnival the way Brazilians do with their elaborate Mardi Gras–type activities, the city of Ambato in the Andean highlands is famous for its Feria de las Flores y de la Fruta (Fair of Flowers and Fruit) that coincides with Carnival. Because the Monday and Tuesday of Carnival are often a national holiday, many Ecuadorians visit Ambato to partake in the celebration and enjoy the natural beauty and pleasant climate. Carnival is also a time when many Ecuadorians and tourists visit the country's beaches.

One of Ecuador's most popular fiestas is on New Year's Eve. During the day of December 31, many cities and towns have public displays of large puppet-like figures, called *años viejos*, that symbolize the old year. These figures are frequently satirical depictions of well-known politicians and civic leaders. At midnight, Ecuadorians burn the *años viejos*, and throughout each city and town a sea of bonfires symbolizes the end of the old year and the beginning of the new.

Generally, families gather for a late dinner of turkey as they greet the New Year together. After midnight, many Ecuadorians go off to private parties or to dance clubs, and celebrate until dawn. As one might expect, January 1 is a day of rest.

Textiles are a favorite at open-air markets. Courtesy of James Hilty.

Otavalo and the Open-Air Markets

Open-air markets have a long tradition in Ecuador. On certain days of the week, many Indians travel from their communities to a central town or city, where they sell and trade the foods they grow or the textiles and handicrafts they make. On market days members of diverse communities, social classes, and ethnic backgrounds come together to interact. Bargaining over prices is a social ritual in which vendors and buyers try to maneuver one another closer to the desired price.

The market at Otavalo is one of Ecuador's most famous; in fact, it has become a standard part of most tourist itineraries. Otavalo lies less than an hour's drive north of Quito, and very early every Saturday morning, crowds of people gather to buy or just to admire the colorful variety of foodstuffs, weavings, textiles, and handicrafts. The atmosphere is festive, and more often than not, the actual buying of things is of secondary importance.

Although supermarkets and shopping centers have long been an important part of Ecuadorian daily life, open-air markets are still thriving throughout the country. In many instances, however, they are adaptations of the one in Otavalo and provide a space for a parallel economy composed of Ecuador's large underemployed population. Contraband and stolen goods of every imaginable sort appear in these venues that the government generally ignores.

A case in point is the section in Guayaquil where one can find a full array of automobile parts and accessories, many of which have been stolen. When one is the victim of a theft, the custom is to go to the auto-parts market and buy back what was lost. Clearly, the city's widespread poverty has created a culture in which many people have accepted the parallel markets as an integral part of national life, or at least as a necessary evil.

RESPONSES TO THE EVILS OF POVERTY

Theft is so pervasive in Ecuador that everything is literally nailed down or fenced in. Iron bars adorn windows and doors. Private homes are generally enclosed by high cement walls that are topped with large pieces of broken glass as a deterrent to would-be thieves. Armed guards are a routine fixture in most public places.

Although poverty, corruption, and violence form a seemingly endless vicious cycle, Ecuadorians continue to find the strength to avoid despair. Notwithstanding their anger at leaders who have been unable to improve the general quality of life, they have learned to improvise and to create their own temporary solutions to long-standing problems. The parallel markets are, in no small measure, an expression of ingenuity and the will to work.

Most Ecuadorians are hardworking people. In the absence of jobs, many turn to the streets as roaming vendors who hawk their wares on the street corners; others line the sidewalks, where they peddle everything from fresh fruit to trinkets. Instead of despair, one frequently senses an almost festive atmosphere; the peddlers actively engage passersby with sales pitches that are often humorous. Although officially unemployed, it is clear that these individuals have created jobs where none existed.

One encounters the same ingenuity in neighborhoods where basic public services such as garbage collection and street maintenance are not adequately provided by the local authorities. Residents often organize weekend *mingas* (volunteer group projects) that recall the indigenous tradition of cooperative and voluntary efforts to carry out necessary community projects. In effect, the *mingas* are another example of Ecuadorians creating alternatives and doing for themselves.

Public protests against inadequate services and myriad social abuses are common in Ecuador. All kinds of groups frequently march through the streets with banners and placards while chanting their particular cause. These

Street vendor preparing fresh fruit drinks in Guayaquil.
Courtesy of James Hilty.

street demonstrations are yet another indication of just how active Ecuadorians are in defending their rights and needs.

One of the most pressing needs that Ecuadorians have to deal with is the lack of adequate housing. As an unending stream of people migrate to the major cities in search of greater opportunities, squatter settlements and colonies spring up almost overnight on the surrounding hills or on the outskirts of such urban centers as Guayaquil and Quito. In the absence of government control and protection, Ecuador's poor take matters into their own hands. Vacant lots, and even recently finished public housing projects that are still unoccupied, are taken over by the squatters, who are frequently referred to as *invasores* (invaders). Once in possession of the lots or buildings, they usually become de facto owners of the property since government officials are

Young girl selling lottery tickets. Courtesy of James Hilty.

reluctant to remove them by force. The government's position is actually quite practical; its apparent openness and tolerance are the result of its inability to offer other solutions to the country's housing shortage.

The *invasores* are a reminder of just how chaotic urban growth is in Ecuador. The lack of planned growth creates a crisis in public services and in health care; squatters frequently live without potable water and adequate protection against such diseases as cholera and typhoid. Thus, many of the poor's solutions to Ecuador's myriad problems have long-term effects that only exacerbate an already deteriorating situation.

People from rural areas or small towns have long believed that the country's principal urban centers are a land of milk and honey. It is no wonder that most Ecuadorians now live in cities. Thus, a predominantly rural culture has been replaced by an urban one. Among the social consequences of such a demographic change is the juxtaposition of overcrowded cities and under-populated rural areas.

Migration patterns have transformed Ecuadorian life. Sprawling cities with their attendant social problems have changed the dynamics of social relationships and the workplace. The greater distances that urban residents have to travel between home and work, for example, have practically destroyed the traditional work schedule, which included about a two-hour break for most people to return home for a large lunch and brief siesta before returning to work in the late afternoon. Today's single shift, from 8 to 4 or 9 to 5, has been accompanied by an increasing number of fast food restaurants and a more hurried lifestyle. The traditional family midday meal has all but disappeared on weekdays.

City growth has also affected the status of the downtown areas, which were the traditional centers of urban life in Ecuador. Although government and major business offices continue to be located downtown, larger cities require more branch offices and satellite locations for business and government. Furthermore, whereas downtown used to be the most prestigious location for one's residence, there is now a marked preference for more isolated subdivisions called *ciudadelas*. These residential areas are very similar to the suburbs in the United States.

These changes, however, should not suggest a total break with past customs and lifestyles. Long and leisurely lunches with family followed by the traditional siesta are still very much a part of weekend living. Also, downtown areas in Ecuador's larger cities continue to be full of life and activity. Unlike their U.S. counterparts, Ecuador's downtown districts generally do not evoke images of the abandoned inner city.

The way tradition and change interact to modify long-standing social customs in Ecuador is not uniform. In fact, Guayaquil and Quito are not necessarily representative of other important cities that have significantly smaller populations. Cuenca, Esmeraldas, Loja, Portoviejo, Ibarra, and Machala, for example, are more likely to retain traditional mores than Guayaquil and Quito. That is not to say that these cities do not suffer from many of the urban problems outlined above or that they continue to live in the remote past. Life in the smaller cities, however, is a reminder of Ecuador's diversity and the extent to which its culture resists generalizations.

PRIVATE VERSUS PUBLIC FACILITIES

In addition to the differences that mark Ecuador's many regions and cities, the inability of the government and its public institutions to provide broad opportunities to the general population has intensified the divisions between the country's social classes. Although Ecuadorians may be admired for their creative responses to the country's dearth of services and facilities, the alternative arrangements embody massive inequalities. In the absence of adequate public funding, the unequal distribution of private resources invariably results in a society of haves and have-nots, with the latter constituting the vast majority of Ecuadorians.

People's responses to the socioeconomic and sociopolitical differences that characterize Ecuador have affected certain social customs. Disparities in the delivery of health care and education, for example, have clearly had an impact on social behavior. Ecuadorians who have the wherewithal avoid public facilities and rarely concern themselves with improving conditions. Understaffed and ill-equipped hospitals, clinics, and schools become non-issues in a society that has created parallel institutions for the haves and have-nots. In such a divided society, civic responsibility tends to be narrow and limited. Alternative and private solutions more often than not create a kind of survival-of-the-fittest mind-set that limits the potential for broad-based community projects.

How else can one explain the proliferation of expensive private universities and junior colleges at the same time that public institutions are in dire need of resources to refurbish deteriorated buildings and to replace outdated equipment? Ecuador is a virtual "tale of two cities" (or two nations). On the one hand, it is characterized by an all-encompassing financial crisis caused by a combination of foreign debt obligations and the natural catastrophes produced by 1998's El Niño; on the other hand, it is dependent upon private investors whose multinational business connections often determine how the government and the country's more privileged groups prioritize their needs. This contrast in resources and Ecuador's ever-growing dependence on international interest groups have widened a profound social schism that has further upset national allegiances and loyalties. Consequently, universities funded by private sources that are linked to multinational interests, for example, are not averse to adopting foreign academic models and programs of study that may have very little relevance to Ecuador's most pressing needs.

The current trend in higher education in Ecuador is to emphasize associate degrees in business fields and computer technology. An impressionable and economically vulnerable middle class has bought into the idea of practical careers that supposedly will lead to well-paying jobs in a short period of time. This new form of pragmatism is understandable at a time when the vast majority of Ecuadorians feels threatened by the country's financial crisis. Whereas medicine, engineering, law, and agronomy were once popular fields of study that offered students an opportunity to climb the proverbial social ladder while contributing to Ecuador's overall development and progress, the current vocationalism signals a more self-centered and individualistic approach to higher education. Research, agricultural extension services, and other traditional fields related to national development have been displaced by fields that are anchored primarily in a globalized service economy.

POPULIST POLITICS

As one might expect, populist political leaders thrive on social divisions and disparities. Indeed, despite the progress made in the democratic process since the election of Jaime Roldós in 1979, Ecuadorian politics continues to be dominated by charismatic politicians and demagogues whose speeches and campaigns target the emotions of the estranged and marginalized masses. With regard to who represents the poor, the government continues to be suspect, and the financially solvent sectors of society are still primarily concerned with their own agenda.

It would be grossly simplistic, however, to suggest that the masses are easily manipulated by strong-willed leaders and demagogues. Ecuador's political system is very much a product of the extended family and *compadrazgo* traditions. The urban poor have learned how to use politics to satisfy their immediate needs. Populist politics is closely related to what is commonly referred to as *clientelismo*—a reciprocal arrangement by which people offer their votes for a specific price, such as housing, jobs, electricity, potable water, paved streets.

Thus, populist leaders who rise to national prominence by claiming to champion the causes of the urban poor and disenfranchised are used by the masses to circumvent an inefficient and unresponsive government. Given the conditions in which they live, the masses astutely offer their allegiance and loyalty to dynamic individuals who are established power brokers in national politics and who promise to provide the poor with their most immediate needs. Naturally, this kind of political modus operandi does not lead to continuity in program development. As political power and influence change hands, the urban masses redefine their support for those leaders who best suit their interests.

SOCCER MADNESS

Despite all the social and economic problems that Ecuadorians must confront, and notwithstanding the many obstacles that sharply separate the country's social classes and ethnic groups, soccer madness is one aspect of

Ecuadorian life that everyone seems to share. Ecuadorians closely follow their favorite professional soccer teams. Sunday is game day, and the stadiums become major centers of activity and excitement.

In the absence of cheerleaders and halftime shows that characterize football in the United States, many of Ecuador's soccer fans entertain the crowds by playing horns and drums while screaming chants to urge on their favorite teams and players. The most excitement is generated when Ecuadorian teams play soccer clubs from other countries. The rivalries are intense, and the games always carry an element of national pride and honor.

The Copa de Libertadores (Liberators' Cup), the South American Championship, and the qualifying matches for the World Cup feed Ecuador's passion for soccer. Victories over teams from Argentina or Chile are celebrated long into the night, and losses to Colombia or Peru are an excuse to lament Ecuador's inability to establish itself as an international soccer power. To date, Ecuador has never made it to the World Cup, and few players have established themselves at the international level. The exceptions are Alberto Spencer, who played successfully in Uruguay; Alex Aguinaga, who has had a solid playing career in Mexico; and Iván Caviedes, who in 1998 became a starting forward for the Perugia Soccer Club in Italy and, in 1999, accepted a contract to play in Spain. Each of these players has become an icon in Ecuador; at some very basic psychological level, each seems to reassure Ecuadorians that they, too, are capable of being successful beyond their national borders.

Ecuadorians are not just soccer spectators. From a very early age, boys play soccer. On Sundays, it is common to see vacant lots and city streets converted into soccer fields. The most popular soccer game is called *indor*, and despite its similarity to the English word "indoor," it is not played indoors. *Indor* is soccer adapted to the reduced space of the city streets. The ball is usually about the size of a softball, and the goals are frequently two large stones. Streets are blocked off on Sundays, and drivers generally adapt graciously to the improvised changes in the traffic flow.

Although some youngsters may play soccer for their school teams, and others may play on well-kept fields provided by a private club, *indor* does not depend upon formal sponsors or official leagues. Instead, it belongs to the majority of Ecuadorians. That is to say, to the majority of Ecuadorian males. Girls' soccer is still very much the exception in Ecuador. In fact, participation in most sports by girls is sporadic at best.

Besides soccer, the only other sport that is widely played in Ecuador is Ecuadorian-style volleyball. Unlike the Olympic-style game, the Ecuadorian version allows players more freedom to carry or palm the ball. Also, the ball is somewhat heavier, and players frequently use a soccer ball. Like *indor*, Ecuadorian volleyball does not require special club memberships or expensive equipment. It, too, is a people's game, one that is played on vacant lots, city streets, or any other surface that can support two posts with a net.

ECUADORIAN CUISINE

Although Ecuadorians struggle incessantly with the many problems associated with the country's economic dependence, they never seem to lose their lust for life or their joy in eating. Ecuador's cuisine is incredibly diverse, and each region takes pride in its unique dishes. Ecuadorian food reflects primarily Indian, African, and Spanish culinary traditions. Through the centuries, each region has adapted these traditions to the footstuffs produced and cultivated locally.

In general, Ecuadorians eat three meals, with the midday one being the most substantial. Throughout the country, and regardless of the climate, the main meal often starts with soup. Rice, potatoes, and beans are the basic ingredients of Ecuador's cuisine, and it is not unusual to serve all three during the same meal.

There are innumerable recipes using potatoes, plantains, fish, and the country's many fruits. In Esmeraldas, many dishes are prepared with coconut oil; potatoes and corn give the Sierra its distinctive culinary flavors; and fish, seafood, plantains, yucca, and peanut oil characterize much of the Coast's cuisine. Especially popular are *locro* (a thick soup most commonly made from potatoes or corn), *seco de chivo* (slowly cooked rice with chunks of goat meat), *viche de pescado* (a kind of fish bisque with vegetables and yucca), and *tripa mishqui* (tripe). Some people argue that the provinces of Manabí, Azuay, Tungurahua, and Imbabura produce Ecuador's most celebrated dishes and beverages (Pazos 123). Such affirmations, however, are risky in a country as diverse as Ecuador.

Regardless of one's culinary biases, Ecuadorian cuisine does have a common denominator. *Ají*, a condiment used throughout Ecuador, is made from a small red pepper and is served in liquid form. In general, *ají* is much milder than the chili peppers used in the southwestern United States. Ecuadorians add *ají* to their food as most people in the United States add salt and pepper.

Chinese food deserves special mention. At the beginning of the twentieth century, many Asians arrived in Ecuador to work on the construction of the railroad. Since then, a vibrant Asian community has evolved, and its cuisine has become extremely popular. Chinese restaurants, called *chifas*, can be found throughout the country. *Arroz frito* (fried rice) and *chaulafán* (a chicken or beef dish combined with fried rice) are two of the more popular dishes among Ecuadorian diners.

DEATH AND MOURNING

Long processions of people walking to the cemetery to bury a loved one can still be observed occasionally. In the past, it was more common for wakes to be held at home; today, cemeteries provide special rooms where families can receive friends throughout the night before the funeral. Traditionally, cemeteries were characterized by huge stone monuments and mausoleums, particularly for the wealthy. Today, however, the trend is to bury the dead in *jardines*, or memorial gardens, where landscaping has largely replaced the ostentatious tombstones of the past.

Besides the family's official announcement of a loved one's death that is published in the obituary section of the local newspaper, friends and associates express their condolences in the newspaper. Families normally celebrate a memorial service at a local church one month after the death; the first anniversary is observed in similar fashion.

Visits to the cemetery usually last longer than is customary in the United States. Family members take chairs and sit at the grave site, and it is as though the deceased participates in the family outing. While All Souls Day (November 2), Christmas, Easter, and special family dates are the most common days for visits to the cemeteries, Ecuadorians do not require a special reason to spend time with the deceased. In general, women are more involved than men in visiting and caring for the grave site.

CONCLUSION

Although the customs presented here are not specifically Ecuadorian, they create a partial sense of what it means to be Ecuadorian. Obviously, Ecuador's cultural, ethnic, and geographical diversity precludes any possibility of offering an all-inclusive discussion about social customs. Ecuadorian Blacks singing *arrullos* (lullabies) at funeral wakes, Indians celebrating Corpus Christi, women washing clothes in streams, and Amazonian people making offerings to the soil to ensure successful crops are only a few of the many other customs practiced throughout Ecuador.

The underlying constant in any analysis of social customs must necessarily be how society evolves while it abandons, retains, and modifies those customs. In Ecuador, economics is certainly a major driving force behind such adaptations. It is clear that the ingenuity and creativity which Ecuadorians use to

Women still wash clothes on riverbanks in Cuenca. Courtesy of James Hilty.

maintain the delicate balance between tradition and change form the heart and soul of the country's social customs.

REFERENCES

Carvalho-Neto, Paulo de. *Antología del folklore Ecuatoriano.* 2 vols. Quito: Editorial Universitaria, 1964; Cuenca: Editorial Casa de la Cultura Ecuatoriana, 1970.

Harrison, Regina. *Signs, Songs, and Memory in the Andes: Translating Quechua Language and Culture.* Austin: University of Texas Press, 1989.

————. *Entre el tronar épico y el ilanto elegíaco: Simbología Indígena en la poesía Ecuatoriana de los siglos XIX–XX.* Quito: Ediciones Abya-Yala y Universidad Andina Simón Bolívar, 1996.

Pazos B., Julio. *Recetas criollas: Cocinemos lo nuestro.* Quito: Corporación Editora Nacional El Conejo, 1991.

Whitten, Norman E., Jr., ed. *Cultural Transformations and Ethnicity in Modern Ecuador.* Urbana: University of Illinois Press, 1981.

4

Broadcasting and Print Media

Broadcasting and the print media have had a profound effect on Ecuadorian culture. The discovery and dissemination of new ideas, the championing of diverse social and political causes, and the expanding accessibility of information and knowledge have been the media's keystones. In principle, the media have served as a source of democratization; unlike traditional cultural venues that were controlled by and for a select minority (i.e., the church, the literate, and the wealthy), the media have ensured that knowledge and its communication are more inclusive and more accessible.

The print media in Ecuador can trace their origins to the period immediately preceding the Wars of Independence of the early nineteenth century. Also, the growth of newspapers coincided with the Liberal Revolution and the gradual emergence of a middle class in the final years of the nineteenth century and the early years of the twentieth. Broadcasting reached Ecuador in the 1930s, when North American Protestant missionaries accelerated their efforts to find new Christian followers. In each of these periods, Ecuadorians found themselves at a critical crossroads in their history: *criollos* (people of Spanish ancestry born in the Americas) versus Spanish royalists, the disenfranchised versus the oligarchy, Protestant missionaries versus the Catholic Church. As relationships of power and privilege were being challenged, the media were instrumental in modifying the dominant social order.

Despite these origins of change and democratization, the media in Ecuador are characterized by severe limitations that often stifle openness and free expression. The most serious problem is ownership of the media. The vast majority of holdings is in the hands of a small elite of private business groups and consortia: 96.8 percent of radio, 84.6 percent of television, and 94.4 percent of print journalism are privately owned (Grijalva Jiménez 192). Moreover, the formation of monopolies has been especially stifling for democratically inspired media. Because many of the country's principal newspapers, radio stations, and television stations are owned by the same interest groups, the extent to which Ecuador's media are truly free and open is subject to much debate.

With very few exceptions, the media and media coverage in Ecuador tend to be local. There is no newspaper, for example, that reaches a significant reading public outside the city in which it is published. Most television stations are local or regional, and all are located in the country's major cities. Even radio stations are predominantly city-based, and although their broadcasts reach the largest audiences compared with the other media, most radio programming is still very centralized and geared toward local listeners.

As might be expected the problems of limited ownership and highly localized coverage arise largely from Ecuador's economic underdevelopment and nearly five centuries of geographical, social, economic, and political regionalism. It would be a grave mistake, however, to allow these limitations to overshadow the pivotal role that the media have played in Ecuadorian history. Both as an outlet for creative expression and as a more inclusive system of communication than had been the case before independence, the media have provided Ecuadorians with the real possibility of actively determining their own destiny.

PRINT MEDIA

The first printing press was set up in Ecuador by the Jesuits in 1654, at Ambato; a press began to operate in Quito by 1670 (Mora 54). At first, Ecuador's presses produced religious publications, royal orders or edicts, and official records related to the affairs of the colonial government. It was not until 1792 that the seeds of modern-day print journalism were sown. In that year, Eugenio Espejo (1747–1795) published Ecuador's first newspaper, *Primicias de la cultura de Quito* (The First Fruits of Culture from Quito). Although he published only seven issues, the short-lived *Primicias* gave future writers and journalists a model to emulate and cultivate.

Chapter 6 contains a more complete discussion of Espejo and his important contributions to Ecuadorian independence and the beginnings of a national literature. With regard to his role as Ecuador's first journalist, it is important to note that *Primicias* was part of a protonational project conceived to end a colonial system of privilege and exclusion. The very nature of Espejo's publication constituted a challenge to the prevailing social order. Unlike the printed materials produced by the Catholic Church and royal government, *Primicias* offered an alternative view of colonial Ecuador to readers who lived outside the circles of power. Thus, Ecuador's first newspaper was an expression of civil disobedience and iconoclasm.

This first newspaper was more like a collection of a few printed pages written by one individual. In this sense, *Primicias*'s legacy is more pertinent to today's journalists than to the newspaper business per se. In effect, *Primicias* was Espejo (his writings and personal point of view), and although modern newspapers are frequently influenced by market pressures and business decisions that have little to do with the revolutionary Espejo, his vision and objectives have survived as a professional code for writers who practice journalism as a form of public service.

The growth of Ecuador's modern newspapers began in 1884 with the founding of *El Telégrafo* (The Telegraph; Guayaquil). Important daily newspapers that followed were *El Comercio* (The Commerce, 1906; Quito), *El Universo* (The Universe, 1924; Guayaquil), *El Mercurio* (The Mercury, 1924; Cuenca), *El Expreso* (The Express, 1973; Guayaquil), and *Hoy* (Today, 1982; Quito). In 1944, two evening dailies began to appear: *Últimas Noticias* (The Latest News; Quito) and *La Razón* (Reason; Guayaquil). By 1995, Ecuador had 42 newspapers. Guayaquil's *El Universo* has the largest daily circulation, 240,000 papers; Quito's *El Comercio*, with 200,000 papers and *Hoy* with 110,000 round out Ecuador's principal dailies (Saltos and Vázquez 246–247).

Although the most popular sections in today's newspapers tend to deal with sports, local news, classifieds, and crime reports, Espejo's combative style continues to be a constant in the majority of publications (Grijalva Jiménez 195). Regardless of how the newspapers distribute their coverage, polemical reporting and commentary abound. Whether it is politics, economic policies, or professional sports, journalists use their medium to insist that public leaders account for their decisions and actions.

Using the press as a battleground for ideas and ideals has not been limited to Ecuador's established newspapers. Alternative publications have appeared throughout Ecuadorian history, particularly during times of crisis. Because most have been driven by specific issues, they have generally been short-lived. Ecuadorians refer to these publications as the *prensa chica* (small press). While the format of these papers has varied greatly, their combativeness has not. Attacks expressed with irony, satire, and humor fill the *prensa chica*'s pages

(Aguilar Arévalo 221). *Combate* (Combat), *El Látigo* (The Whip), *El Grito* (The Shout), *La Bomba* (The Bomb), and *Barricada* (Barricade) are titles that illustrate the purpose of these publications.

Ecuador's *prensa chica* should not be confused with the sensationalist tabloids characteristic of the United States. First, it is not about profits. Second, its seeming outlandishness and libelous nature are often characterized by ingenious writing. Finally, most publications have appeared as an expression of civil disobedience rather than of gossip and personal insult.

Despite occasional periods of governmental control and even persecution, Ecuador's press has rarely wavered in its defense of freedom of expression. Frequently the *prensa chica*, for example, has sounded a clarion against the closing of a particular newspaper or the detention of a journalist accused of inciting the public to unlawful acts of protest. Official abuse and threats against a free press have always been met with resistance and solidarity by Ecuador's journalists. As a group, they have not allowed governmental policies to undermine the basic principles that Eugenio Espejo established in 1792 (Aguilar Arévalo 223).

The real danger to a free press in Ecuador has come from the economic sector that controls production and distribution. Limiting the availability of paper and other necessary materials, or tying up such resources until editors satisfy certain conditions, can be more coercive than any threat posed by dictators or authoritarian regimes (Aguilar Arévalo 223–224). As punishment for journalists who use their publications to defend the rights of colleagues whose safety and physical well-being are threatened by despotic leaders, newspaper closings, exile, and even death are measures visible to all; financial control (or blackmail in the most extreme cases), on the other hand, is not so easily seen.

Notwithstanding the many pressures that can compromise a free press, journalism in Ecuador has become increasingly specialized with the emergence of professional organizations and of academic programs in communications at numerous universities. Most newspapers, however, continue the tradition of incorporating into their ranks distinguished writers and intellectuals with areas of expertise outside of journalism. This relationship is especially true for writers of literature, who have long used newspapers and magazines as their principal means of expression in Ecuador. In fact, it is not uncommon for Ecuadorians to speak of journalism as a literary genre (Aguilar Arévalo 218).

Throughout the history of Ecuador's print media, so-called high culture has always managed to find a place for itself in newspapers and magazines. At times, publishers have reserved a daily column for a distinguished writer;

at other times, an entire page called the *página literaria* (literary page) has come out weekly so that readers can keep abreast of the most recent developments in both Ecuadorian and foreign literature. In the best of times, important newspapers have published weekly literary and cultural supplements of a dozen or more pages. Considering the wide circulation of newspapers in comparison with the very limited editions of most published books in Ecuador, one can appreciate the allure that literary supplements have frequently had for many writers who have struggled unsuccessfully to reach a large readership.

For the most part, the space that publishers and editors set aside for literature and the arts was intended for a highly educated and sophisticated public. Occasionally, however, the literary and cultural material that appeared in the newspapers was the product of a more ambitious project than providing for an elite's reading pleasure. Depending upon who was in charge of the selection of materials, the literary and cultural column/page/supplement was an attempt to integrate high culture more broadly into Ecuadorian daily life.

Many of those responsible for selecting the cultural materials understood that their role was to train readers to be more informed and discerning. Great care was taken to publish high-quality texts that had been written by the most accomplished writers from Ecuador and abroad. A cursory look at some of the works published in the literary sections reveals a virtual "who's who" of literature. Besides many well-known national writers who will be discussed in Chapter 6, readers were able to read selections by such international luminaries of the past and present as Rubén Darío (Nicaragua), Antonio Machado (Spain), Federico García Lorca (Spain), Pablo Neruda (Chile), Octavio Paz (Mexico), Gabriel García Márquez (Colombia), Franz Kafka (Czechoslovakia), Jean Paul Sartre (France), and Charles Baudelaire (France).

The literary sections included discussions and commentaries about literature and its role in society. Basically, writers were committed to demonstrating to the broad spectrum of newspaper readers that literature need not be confined to the proverbial ivory tower. Printing literature in newspapers was tantamount to joining two traditionally disparate forms of expression, high culture and mass media. While one can question the extent to which the literary pages actually produced new readers, there is no doubt that writers had found a medium offering them the possibility of interacting more closely with a broader reading public.

El Meridiano Cultural (The Cultural Meridian) clearly illustrates the role that a cultural supplement can play in journalism. Published weekly in Guayaquil's *Meridiano*, its first issue appeared in August 1983, under the direction of Fernando Artieda and Carlos Calderón Chico. Unlike many of its counterparts that were satisfied with offering readers an array of good literature, *El Meridiano Cultural* was determined to be more than a potpourri of reading materials. Readers needed direction and context in order to understand literature's social and historical importance more fully. To that end, *El Meridiano Cultural* published literary texts by renowned Ecuadorian and Latin American writers who had championed justice and freedom. Reading was to be more than innocent recreation; it was intended to deepen one's commitment to contributing actively to a more just and humane society.

El Meridiano Cultural sought to bring together Ecuador's highly stratified society. The supplement's pages juxtaposed articles and photographs that exalted the value and importance of both high culture and popular culture. Articles about Shakespeare appeared beside photographs of Indian artisans; ballet and salsa were treated as equally valuable forms of dance; through photographs, drawings, and articles, the supplement offered a portrait of Ecuador's poor that was never patronizing or condescending. In effect, its careful selection and presentation of materials enabled *El Meridiano Cultural* to create among its readers a sense of interaction rather than one of division or separatism.

Although a change in the newspaper's editorial priorities led to the eventual demise of *El Meridiano Cultural,* the supplement's issues demonstrated that the mass media do not have to "dumb down" material to be popular among readers. To be sure, many periodicals have catered to the general public's supposed desire for self-gratification and superficiality by celebrating the latest fashions or by idolizing movie stars. Under the direction of Artieda and Calderón, however, *El Meridiano Cultural* nurtured critical thinking and consciousness-raising in a format and language that embraced all readers.

Besides daily newspapers and their literary or cultural supplements, Ecuador's print media include a plethora of popular and specialized magazines devoted to myriad topics. The two publications that come closest to reaching a national readership are *Vistazo* (Look) and *Estadio* (Stadium). Unlike most publications, which rarely circulate beyond their place of origin or outside a particular circle of initiated readers, *Vistazo* and *Estadio* are found throughout the country. Because soccer is arguably Ecuador's principal pastime, it is not surprising that a soccer magazine such as *Estadio* would be so popular. Moreover, its broad-based circulation appears to be due to the monopolistic nature of Ecuador's media and to the fact that *Estadio,* published since 1962, has no real competition capable of reaching the country's avid soccer fans.

Vistazo, which began circulating in 1957, is published by the same media group that owns *Estadio.* One of *Vistazo*'s most notable features is its front cover, which always spotlights a beautiful woman in a bathing suit. Notwithstanding the sexual allure and attendant expectations that such photographs might generate at the newsstand (i.e., trashy cover stories about promiscuity and sexual fantasies), this biweekly magazine actually covers topics ranging from national politics to human interest stories. Clearly, the gratuitous photographs of scantily clad women on *Vistazo*'s front cover are a promotional gimmick. In effect, while *Vistazo*'s wide appeal in Ecuador is due in no small measure to its ability to address the diverse interests of readers throughout the country, its success has been the result of savvy marketing strategies that have defined print journalism as entertainment and business. Unlike its counterparts, *Vistazo* has developed a comprehensive mission that includes mass production, promotion, and distribution.

As one might expect, computer technologies and Internet connections have had a profound effect on Ecuador's print media. Unlike the past, when newspapers and magazines were dependent upon a few news agencies for most of the material published about foreign events and people, today's media have been able to expand their coverage and become less provincial than in the past. More important, the Internet has enabled Ecuador's principal periodicals to circulate beyond their traditional boundaries. Some useful websites for those interested in reading about Ecuador's current events are www.bacan.com; www.eluniverso.com; www.hoy.com.ec; www4.ecua.net.ec.

RADIO

In comparison with the print media and television, radio has the broadest distribution and delivery network in Ecuador's mass communication system. By 1995, there were 311 AM stations and 251 FM stations. Each province has at least one FM station and no fewer than two AM stations (Saltos and Vázquez 245–246). For the most part, radio programs are of national origin and are produced either at the radio stations or at other sites in Ecuador (Grijalva Jiménez 193). While television's sphere of influence tends to remain in the country's urban centers, radio is the principal means of mass communication in rural Ecuador. The affordability and abundant supply of transistor radios have made radio increasingly accessible to larger audiences than those of the other media.

Ecuador's first radio broadcast occurred in 1931. The World Radio Missionary Fellowship founded HCJB Radio, The Voice of the Andes, which became "the first evangelical radio station to operate outside of the United

States" (Goffin 41). Although HCJB began modestly with a transmitter of no more than 250 watts, by 1981 it had become the most widely broadcast missionary station in the world (Mora 75).

Whereas HCJB emphasized religious programming, the growing number of stations that have emerged since 1931 have shown a preference for entertainment and news programs. By the mid-1990s, entertainment made up 55 percent of radio broadcasts in Ecuador, and news and information occupied 26 percent of air-time (Grijalva Jiménez 193). The most popular entertainment programs on radio are music shows, broadcasts targeted especially to women and children, and call-in shows. For the news and information programs, most of the airtime is devoted to local and national news, sports, and opinion-oriented shows (Grijalva Jiménez 194).

Because of the proliferation of radio stations in Ecuador, it has been impossible to control program quality. Also, the vast majority of stations are privately owned, and the business interests of the sponsors tend to dictate the kinds of programs that are aired (Hurtado 199). Radio HCJB has been an exception; its broadcasts have avoided the light and superficial material of most stations. Its programs have a definite Evangelical agenda that appeals to a particular group of listeners.

The *Escuelas Radiofónicas Populares* (People's Radio Schools) are another example of radio stations that have not been driven by profits. Established in 1962 by the late Archbishop Leonidas Proaño, the Radio Schools were an integral part of a literacy campaign in Chimborazo province. By 1969, there were 111 such schools with some 900 students. The program eventually spread to eight provinces in the Sierra, three on the Coast, and four in the Amazon Basin. The archbishop's goal was to have 3,000 Radio Schools by 1971 that would be served by a radio station capable of reaching listeners in the entire country (Hurtado 199).

Many radio programs offer cultural and educational spots. Most are aired thanks to the interest and initiative of broadcasters or station managers who are willing to break from their station's set agenda. Frequently, when these individuals leave their posts, the programming innovations are replaced by programs reflecting the likes and dislikes of the new broadcasting staff. Be that as it may, cultural and educational programs account for a mere 7 percent of Ecuadorian radio airtime (Grijalva Jiménez 193).

TELEVISION

The first complete television broadcast in Ecuador occurred in 1959 when The Voice of the Andes branched out to become The Window of the Andes.

Radio HCJB and its missionaries had sought a license for two television stations in Ecuador since 1957. Between 1959 and 1962, much public controversy surrounded HCJB's attempts to expand its radio activities into television. Because of HCJB's professed Evangelical objectives, many Ecuadorian groups opposed giving the Protestant organization an even stronger foothold in the media for its religious message (Mora 80).

Initially, the Ecuadorian government granted HCJB its license with the proviso that it regularly broadcast news and information about special events. In return, HCJB would be allowed to offer religious programs (Mora 90). During its first decade, HCJB-TV in Quito (Channel 4) launched a formidable evangelical campaign that aired numerous internationally renowned preachers and ministers whose programs lasted as long as one hour (Mora 95). Channel 4 was so successful that several Ecuadorian entrepreneurs decided to experiment with television as a medium that might suit their business interests. Thus, in 1960, a commercial station was organized in Guayaquil (Channel 4), and it began broadcasting in 1965. Commercial television was established in Quito in 1961 (Channel 6), and its broadcasts began airing in 1964 (Mora 101–102).

As in most parts of the world, the arrival of television in Ecuador brought profound changes in people's daily lives. Television introduced new forms of entertainment, it created new social habits, it ushered in a demand for new technologies, and it opened the way for new professions and careers (Mora 161). In fact, Ecuadorian television established a whole new industry that required everything from studio technicians and production experts to sales personnel and television repairmen.

At the beginning, Ecuador depended primarily upon foreign professionals to establish, install, and organize its television industry. The Ecuadorians who were involved in television in the early years usually came from other media or were individuals who had had successful careers in public relations. With respect to programming, stations relied heavily on films imported from the United States, Mexico, and Argentina. Newscasts were done live, and due to the high costs of videotape, television reporting was supplemented by photographs and guest commentators (Mora 102–103). Initially, Guayaquil's Channel 4 and Quito's Channel 6 aired their telecasts from 4:00 P.M. until 9:30 P.M. By 1969, the stations had expanded their programming schedules to run from 12:45 P.M. until 11:45 P.M. (As of 1999, along with a significant increase in stations, airtime had expanded from 5:45 A.M. until 1:30 A.M.)

The year 1978 was a benchmark for Ecuadorian television. The owners of Guayaquil's Channel 2, which had been founded in 1967 and had become Ecuador's second major commercial television station, formed Ecuavisa. This private company was the first attempt to consolidate broadcasting efforts between stations in different cities. Specifically, the central idea behind Ecuavisa was for Guayaquil's Channel 2 and Quito's Channel 8 to share their personnel and resources in an effort to offer programming that would reach beyond a local viewing audience. Although the original Ecuavisa consortium was formally dissolved in 1981, Channels 2 of Guayaquil and 8 of Quito signed an agreement in 1982 to continue sharing resources for their afternoon and evening newscasts (Mora 135).

Besides signaling the potential for developing national television networks in Ecuador, Ecuavisa reflected the trend to create monopolies in the media and communications. The principal newspapers, radio stations, and television stations are owned by about half a dozen business groups whose economic, social, and political influence continues to determine the flow of information and programming in all of the media, especialy in television (Saltos and Vázquez 245). The high costs associated with the television industry make it almost impossible for small or midsized business groups to compete with the large corporations. To be sure, the problems of financial influence and control are not unique to Ecuador. However, in a small country like Ecuador, where opportunities and resources are severely limited under even the best of circumstances, the power of monopolies can be absolute.

Ecuadorian television is concentrated primarily in Quito and Guayaquil. Of Ecuador's 28 stations, 10 are in Quito and 10 in Guayaquil (Saltos and Vázquez 245). The principal networks with national coverage are Gamavisión (Quito), Teleamazonas (Quito), Telesistema (Quito), Ecuavisa (Quito), and TC Televisión (Guayaquil); there are another seven stations with regional broadcasting capability: Telerama (Cuenca), Corporación Ecuatoriana TV (Guayaquil), Tele Cuatro (Guayaquil), Americ.Visión (Guayaquil), Perone S.A. (Guayaquil), Asomavisión (Quito), and Telesucesos (Quito). The rest of Ecuador's television stations are strictly for local audiences; outside of Quito and Guayaquil, there are stations in Cuenca, Machala, Esmeraldas, Ibarra, Loja, Portoviejo, and Ambato (Saltos and Vázquez 244–245).

In some respects, little has changed since the early days of commercial television. Programming continues to be dominated by foreign shows, which make up 57.66 percent of the material aired on Ecuadorian television (Grijalva Jiménez 195). Most televised programs still fall into the light entertainment category: soap operas, musical and variety shows, game shows, cartoons, feature movies, and popular TV series from the United States. As was true in the past, news and information constitute the other major programming category. Newscasts are aired from 6:00 A.M. until 8:30 A.M.; from 12:30 P.M. until 2:00 P.M.; from 7:00 P.M. until 8:00 P.M.; and from 11:00 P.M. until midnight.

Soap operas are one of the most popular types of program on Ecuadorian television. Most soaps are broadcast in the evenings, and they do not go on indefinitely. The majority come from Mexico, Venezuela, and Brazil, and they are the same soap operas viewed by audiences throughout Latin America. Love affairs, mistaken identities, intrigue, machismo, and women as sexual objects are some of the most popular themes.

Of Ecuador's leading television networks, Ecuavisa has been the one most committed to creating national programs other than newscasts or variety shows. In contrast with the pervasiveness of North American movies and Latin American soaps, Ecuavisa has sponsored numerous projects that have given Ecuadorian writers, directors, and actors an opportunity to showcase their talents. Especially noteworthy have been its made-for-television movies based on such Ecuadorian novels as *Cumandá* and *El chulla Romero y Flores* (these will be discussed in Chapter 6). *El ángel de piedra* (The Angel of Stone) was a highly successful 1989 soap opera whose cast and production staff consisted primarily of Ecuadorians.

Although Ecuador's first attempt at producing its own soap opera followed quite closely the genre's themes of intrigue and romance, the public enjoyed listening to Ecuadorian Spanish (as opposed to that of Venezuela, for example) and watching the drama unfold in Ecuador's highlands. *El ángel de piedra* followed the plight of a young boy who cannot accept his widowed mother's remarriage. Because he clings to the memory of the sculptor he assumes was his father, the relationship with his stepfather is strained, at best. To make matters worse, upon the mother's sudden death, his stepfather decides to marry a woman with four children who continually mistreat the young orphan. In desperation, he runs away from his stepfamily, who, with the passing of time, assume the boy has disappeared forever.

In some ways, *El ángel de piedra* is reminiscent of Alexandre Dumas' nineteenth-century novel *The Count of Monte Cristo*. After a long absence, the young man returns to take vengeance against his stepfamily. Assuming a different identity for each situation, he goes about destroying the lives of his step-siblings; in each case, his deception undermines the reputations and social position he believes should have been his. The soap's climax occurs when the last sibling to be punished foils the protagonist's plan by discovering his real identity. More important, however, is the revelation that the stepfather was in fact the young man's biological father. All ends as the main character, frustrated and disillusioned, destroys a statue of an angel sculpted by the man he believed to be his father.

The outstanding camera work, the interesting script, and the suggestive ending that characterized *El ángel de piedra* offered Ecuadorians a polished production that demonstrated the artistic heights to which they could rise if given adequate resources and opportunities. Notwithstanding the viewers' enthusiastic response to *El ángel de piedra* and Ecuavisa's other programming initiatives, few sponsors have been willing to invest consistently in costly national productions. And, of course, television is financially dependent upon sponsors. Consequently, profits and marketing decisions largely determine programming. Moreover, because the allure of North American culture is so strong among television viewers, there are few incentives to broadcast anything other than cost-effective imports that generally showcase four basic motifs: individualism, consumerism, violence, and multiple expressions of discrimination (Saltos and Vázquez 245).

The availability of cable television, especially in Guayaquil and Quito, is another obstacle that has undermined efforts to develop national programs and talent. The seemingly endless array of programs and shows renders futile any plan to compete with slick and well-packaged imports (e.g., *Beverly Hills 90210, Melrose Place, Cosby Show, The X-Files, Baywatch*). Thus, television programming that could be the genuine creation and expression of Ecuadorians continues to be elusive as sponsors limit local efforts to newscasts and to variety shows that have minimal overhead costs. Actors, actresses, writers, directors, and costume designers, for example, are still very peripheral to the television industry in Ecuador.

One can justifiably lament the dearth of original programs and challenging opportunities that characterizes television in Ecuador (and that of so many other places in the world, including the United States). However, there have been entertainment and information shows created and produced by Ecuadorians that have attempted to be more culturally and educationally responsible than those most commonly aired. An important example is Freddy Ehlers's show, *La Televisión*, which is broadcast nationally by Gamavisión each Sunday at 9:00 P.M. Although North Americans would probably describe Ehlers's program as a mix of *60 Minutes* and *20/20, La Televisión* is not just about reporting or presenting controversial issues. Ehlers frequently uses his prime-time TV show as a catalyst for community action. As topics of national importance, such as the environment, Indian rights, and privatization, are analyzed and commented upon, Ehlers's informal and conversational style creates a special rapport with many viewers, who feel challenged to take a stand and to become actively engaged in working for social change. In fact, Ehlers's communication skills and television popularity are such that he was twice a prominent presidential candidate during the 1990s.

Freddy Ehlers and *La Televisión* clearly illustrate just how powerful and persuasive television is in Ecuador. Although the medium is still primarily urban, concentrated in Quito and Guayaquil, television reportedly reaches

90 percent of Ecuadorians (Saltos and Vázquez 248). Thus, it is not surprising that governments routinely purchase airtime to highlight their activities and accomplishments as a basic means of maintaining public support. Unfortunately, however, because television continues to depend upon commercial groups for its financing, publicity and advertisements frequently seem to overshadow everything else that is broadcast. In fact, about 45 percent of the advertising in Ecuador is on television, and more than half of the television commercials made in Ecuador are produced abroad, especially in Colombia and Chile (Saltos and Vázquez 248).

There are still too few studies on television viewing habits in Ecuador to draw firm conclusions on the long-term effects that television has had on Ecuadorians. A casual observation of households, however, would probably indicate that a "couch-potato" culture is still not pervasive. Certainly, television has affected the quality of interactions among people. TV means there is less time for leisurely after-dinner conversations or parlor games. Nevertheless, because Ecuador is such a gregarious society, one that places such a premium on socializing, television viewing is not yet as vital to daily life there as it is in the United States.

REFERENCES

Aguilar Arévalo, Eugenio. "El periodismo en los 150 años de vida republicana." *In Arte y cultura. Ecuador: 1830–1980*. Ed. Luis Mora Ortega. Quito: Corporación Editora Nacional, 1980. 215–227.

Carrión, Alejandro. "El ensayo periodístico en Espejo, Solano y Montalvo." *In Arte y cultura. Ecuador: 1830–1980*. Ed. Luis Mora Ortega. Quito: Corporación Editora Nacional, 1980. 233–248.

Goffin, Alvin M. *The Rise of Protestant Evangelism in Ecuador, 1895–1990*. Gainesville: University Press of Florida, 1994.

Grijalva Jiménez, Agustín, ed. *Datos básicos de la realidad nacional*. Quito: Corporación Editora Nacional, 1996.

Hurtado, Oswaldo. *Dos mundos superpuestos: Ensayo de diagnóstico de la realidad ecuatoriana*. Quito: INEDES, 1969.

Mora, Alba Luz. *La televisión en el Ecuador*. Guayaquil: Editorial Amauta, 1982.

Saltos G., Napoleón, and Lola Vázquez, eds. *Ecuador: Su realidad*. 5th ed. Quito: Fundación "José Peralta," 1997.

5

Cinema

Although Ecuadorians have long been avid moviegoers, filmmaking has never received the broad attention and financial support that are so essential for the development of the cinema as an art form and as a viable industry. Besides those who distribute films (most of which are imports) and those who own movie theaters, few Ecuadorians have been able to earn a living from the cinema. Their commitment to and love for movies give filmmakers, actors, and actresses the energy and resolve to practice their art despite a general lack of resources.

Due to the absence of a profitable or highly visible film industry, very few people are aware of the existence of a national cinema that has interpreted and documented many key aspects of twentieth-century Ecuador. In fact, along with Ecuador's socially engaged writers and painters, many practitioners of the cinema have been instrumental in elaborating a pluralistic and complex portrait of Ecuador. Much of this history is now accessible to the general public thanks to the work that Ecuador's Cinemateca Nacional (National Film Archive and Library) has sponsored since its founding in 1981.

THE CINEMATECA NACIONAL

Under the steadfast and creative leadership of Ulises Estrella, the Cinemateca Nacional has made significant progress toward creating an infrastructure of public awareness, interest, and support for Ecuadorian film and filmmaking. It is the only institution in Ecuador that is dedicated to the preservation and promotion of the country's motion pictures; it encourages and sponsors research programs as well as film festivals and symposia. Much of the Cinemateca's work has been inspired by its participation in such international organizations as the Federación Internacional de Archivos de Filmes (International Federation of Film Archives) and the Coordinadora Latino-americana de Archivos de Filmes (Latin American Coordinating Council for Film Archives). The Cinemateca is a living film archive that combines interest in the past with commitment to the future.

The Cinemateca is a well-rounded center for cinema studies. On the one hand, its research and archival projects have created a vital collection of national (and international) films and videos; on the other hand, the Cinemateca has assembled a critical mass of historical and cultural sources that supplement the film library and illustrate the extent to which cinema has been an integral part of an evolving national culture in search of its identity. Many of the Cinemateca's special educational programs for children and school-teachers have been made possible by funding from such international organizations as UNESCO and the International Federation of Film Archives.

Because the Cinemateca is a division within the Casa de la Cultura Ecuatoriana (Ecuador's House of Culture), its mission has gained significantly more visibility and legitimacy than most private and independent groups devoted to cinema studies and filmmaking. Furthermore, with nearly six decades of experience as the country's principal cultural center, charged with a broad range of artistic and scientific activities, the Casa de la Cultura Ecuatoriana has guaranteed the Cinemateca's stability and continuity. Consequently, program development and long-range planning have been central to the Cinemateca's missions of preservation, research, and education.

THE EARLY DAYS

To reconstruct the history of film and filmmaking in Ecuador, one must go back to 1874, when the German scientist Theodore Wolf introduced Ecuadorian audiences to the *linterna mágica* (magical lantern), a projector that he used to present still images of European cities. By the beginning of the twentieth century, a growing number of Ecuadorians were viewing moving pictures. These early films lacked a fixed sequence of events or a chronological development of themes, however, and thus they were more reminiscent of Wolf's *linterna mágica* than the motion pictures that had begun to captivate European audiences. Many Ecuadorians were first exposed to the early films while attending shows held in huge tents. It was not unusual for some of the audiences to sit behind the screen, watching a turned-around version of the movie.

The first moving pictures made in Ecuador date to 1906, when an Italian businessman and cinematographer, Carlo Valenti, filmed firefighters and a Corpus Christi procession in Guayaquil. Valenti had brought with him from Europe numerous films that he presented in Guayaquil and Quito. Although Valenti had been preceded by entrepreneurs who had introduced Ecuadorians to motion pictures, he was the first to utilize Ecuador and Ecuadorians as film subjects. The appeal of cinema was greatly intensified when audiences began to see themselves and their friends on the movie screen.

At first, film exhibitors were limited to the venues that each town or city had available for movie showings. Once the public's interest in watching movies had been piqued, however, and the number of films and film exhibitors had begun to outgrow Ecuador's limited supply of theaters, film distributing companies started building their own locales. The growing competition among exhibitors who were seeking their niche in an expanding market of moviegoers mushroomed with the creation of Ecuador's merchant marine in 1913 and the opening of the Panama Canal in 1914. As film imports began to arrive steadily and abundantly, movies became big business in Ecuador.

The popularity of the early films affected many of Ecuador's social mores and customs. Going to the movies quickly became a major social event that for many Ecuadorians eventually was as much a part of daily life as attending to one's business and religious affairs. In fact, by 1914, the Catholic Church and many self-proclaimed moralists began to campaign against the cinema. Although these so-called champions of decency and tradition condemned what they perceived to be the licentious nature of many of the period's silent movies, it is clear that they were reacting against a new medium that had already begun to transform long-standing social values. As might be expected, such a transformation implied a reevaluation of which members of society best represented the public's interests and needs.

By the 1920s, the public's fascination and identification with the movies were complete. Film distributors and exhibitors were among the first to recognize just how persuasive and influential film had become. As the public emulated what it saw on screen, it began to demand new living conditions and opportunities. The gas stoves, Victrolas, cosmetics, fashions, and modern sanitary installations that appeared on the movie screens created a growing demand among Ecuadorians for such amenities. In fact, the allure of such images was so powerful that many Ecuadorians began to assign greater social status to people who were capable of reproducing the lifestyles they saw on screen.

It was not long before some business groups and government agencies used film to communicate their respective messages to both a national and an international audience that was spellbound by motion pictures. Thus, the 1920s saw a dramatic increase in local movie production by these agencies. Films were made in the hopes of drawing international attention to Ecuador and thus attracting foreign investment.

The local film production that began in earnest in the 1920s was not limited to economics or politics, however. People interested in ethnography, history, literature, and the arts also turned to film. In 1924, Augusto San Miguel made the first Ecuadorian film of fiction. *El tesoro de Atahualpa* (Atahualpa's Treasure) was an adaptation of a legend about Atahualpa, the last Inca, who shortly before his death in the early sixteenth century supposedly hid an immense treasure of gold from the Spanish conquerors. The film follows a young medical student who befriends an old and ailing Indian in exchange for a map showing the location of the treasure.

San Miguel was a true filmmaking pioneer. With continued financial backing from the Ecuador Film Company, in 1925 he brought to the screen his *Un abismo y dos almas* (An Abyss and Two Souls). This silent film openly denounced the cruel treatment and the many injustices suffered by the country's Indians who still lived in captivity on estates that belonged to greedy landowners. San Miguel understood that film could be an effective expression of social realism. Just as many of his contemporaries had done in literature and the visual arts, he initiated a social protest tradition that continues to characterize many of the best works in Ecuadorian cinema.

ECUADOR'S MODERN CINEMA

Although the 1920s is considered the "golden age" of Ecuadorian cinema, few filmmakers and producers in Ecuador had the wherewithal to make the transition from silent movies to talkies. The ever-growing technology and equipment needs consolidated Ecuador's dependence on film imports; thus, most Ecuadorians were conditioned to think of the cinema almost entirely in terms of being passive spectators. Even those who participated in the creative process of film production could not escape the realities of dependence. Many of the films made prior to the 1980s were coproductions with international film companies in which Ecuador supplied the scenery and some of the cast while the foreign partners provided the rest (Muñoz Martineaux 38).

The prohibitive costs of elaborate feature films that dominated international markets in the 1940s and 1950s did not deter Ecuadorian filmmakers from being creative. Instead of imitating Hollywood-type productions, they continued working within the documentary film tradition that had been so vital to creating a record and a memory of significant aspects of Ecuadorian history and culture. Unfortunately, documentaries rarely interested large audiences, and mainstream movie theaters therefore tended to ignore such films.

By the turbulent 1960s, however, opportunities began to open up for alternative filmmakers, both in Ecuador and in the rest of Latin America. Social revolutions throughout the Americas convinced many that change was essential. Audiences had become too accustomed to formulaic productions in which the spectacle of moviemaking overshadowed all attempts to elaborate meaningful messages that might inspire the public to struggle against social injustice.

Throughout Latin America, a preference arose for films that stripped away the glitter common to highly stylized and overly sanitized studio productions. Young filmmakers sought natural settings, they preferred nonprofessional actors, and they abandoned expensive equipment while producing

> films about and for and eventually with the disenfranchised Latin American masses. They sought to express "national" reality which they believed to be hidden, distorted, or negated by the dominant sectors of the media. . . . These socially conscious filmmakers would eventually take the entire past and present of their countries and their region as their subject matter, probing the privileged as well as the marginalized sectors, examining historical and contemporary as well as invented examples of exploitation and rebellion, complicity and refusal, all in the name of the discovery or recovery of a more authentic national identity. (Burton x-xi)

Latin America's new cinema was to be anchored in the documentary tradition; it would be realist, national, and popular (Burton xi).

These changes illustrate the extent to which Ecuadorian cinema represents an important chapter in the development of Latin American film. One could argue that Latin America's new cinema was really a resurgence of the kind of filmmaking undertaken in the 1920s by such pioneers as San Miguel. The key difference between film production of the past and the modern period, however, has to do with the number of film creators and viewers who were aware of participating in an alternative project characterized by clearly recognizable objectives. Therefore, what was fundamentally experimental and exploratory in the 1920s evolved into a broadly accepted discourse that would unify filmmakers and film enthusiasts throughout Latin America.

The Creation of a Film Culture

With the impetus gained from the successful experiences of other countries in Latin America, Ecuador saw the emergence of a new and larger audience interested in a socially engaged cinema. Unfortunately, few of the mainstream movie theaters were willing to explore new markets, and thus it was imperative to create parallel spaces in which younger audiences could cultivate a new film culture. One of the important outcomes of such a project was the gradual development of an environment that encouraged Ecuadorian filmmakers to continue producing socially responsible films.

Progressive film enthusiasts understood that filmmaking would not flourish in Ecuador without a corps of enlightened and demanding viewers. Thus, beginning in 1956, the *cine club* (film-viewing club) became a popular mechanism to train audiences in the art of watching movies. The Casa de la Cultura Ecuatoriana in Quito was among the first to sponsor such a club under the direction of Jorge Enrique Adoum, one of Ecuador's foremost poets and novelists.

By the 1960s, *cine clubs* had attracted a large following throughout the country. In 1964, the Cine Club Cultural was founded in Quito; during its gatherings, audiences viewed European films by such progressive filmmakers as Federico Fellini and Michelangelo Antonioni. The club's sessions also included debates and public discussions about the material. In 1967, the Central University in Quito established its Cine Club Universitario under the leadership of Ulises Estrella, poet and future director of the Cinemateca Nacional. This club's initial sessions offered a retrospective view of German expressionism and silent films. Later, it sponsored a full week of movies dedicated to the *cine joven español* (young Spanish cinema). More important, the club had 1,500 members who participated in the scheduled discussions and symposia. The Cine Club Universitario also distributed a publication devoted to cinema.

The oil boom of the 1970s was certainly propitious for the continued development of a solid foundation for Ecuador's cinema. In 1971, the Central University of Quito converted its Teatro Universitario (University Theater) into the country's first movie theater dedicated exclusively to showing nonmainstream films. Later, the Central University altered the structure of its Cine Club Universitario to create an academic department of cinema studies and filmmaking. Ulises Estrella was selected as the department's director. Clearly, this university initiative was the seed for the creation of the Cinemateca Nacional in 1981.

The year 1977 was a watershed one for Ecuadorian cinema. Two television networks (Channel 8 of Quito and Channel 2 of Guayaquil) sponsored a contest for short films. In September, a private organization of Ecuadorian filmmakers was established (Asociación de Autores Cinematográficos del Ecuador); this group's principal mission was to create incentives and opportunities for filmmaking in Ecuador.

After twenty years of cultivating *cine clubs* and other cinema-related activities, Ecuador had made great strides in establishing an atmosphere conducive to the production side of cinema. In 1979, the Central University's Film Department organized the Primer Encuentro Nacional de Cineastas (First National Meeting of Filmmakers). For four days, participants came together to analyze and evaluate films that had been made during the previous five years and that dealt with national themes of a social, anthropological, and ethnographic nature. In December, Ecuadorian filmmakers participated in Havana's annual Festival Internacional del Nuevo Cine (International New Cinema Festival). By the 1980s, an increasing number of Ecuadorians were showing their work in competitions and festivals throughout Latin America, the United States, and Europe.

Noteworthy Documentaries Produced Since 1980

Ecuador's newest wave of filmmakers is deeply conscious of its creative roots. Many of the films that began to appear in the 1980s were influenced by the country's documentary films produced in the 1920s and by the socially committed ones that emerged throughout Latin America in the 1960s. As the young filmmakers matured and gained experience with their medium, they experimented with techniques that would allow their principal subjects to participate more actively in the conceptualization and production of the films. Indeed, there was a gradual rejection of the old-style paternalism inherent in those earlier works that were intended to defend the exploited or to speak on behalf of the people being documented. Clearly, Ecuador's filmmakers identified with the growing commitment to democratization that had been inspired by the 1959 revolution in Cuba and the subsequent ones in Nicaragua, Guatemala, and El Salvador. Thus, by the 1980s the need to destroy traditional hierarchies of authority and authorship had become an artistic and social imperative.

Testimonial approaches to filmmaking constitute one of the most distinctive features of Ecuador's new cinema. By allowing the common people the opportunity to represent themselves, both visually and verbally, filmmakers have begun to produce works that are less interpretative and more authentic. In the past, the creative process lauded moviemakers for their ability to re-create the world that was of interest. Filmmakers offered their authorial view of what lies on the other side of the camera lens. With the new cinema, however, creativity was measured in terms of how convincingly the filmmaker could present the dialogue that linked him with his subjects. The camera lens had become a kind of two-way mirror in which the filmmaker and his cast of participants were partners in the creative process. In principle, this kind of collaboration was meant to give the voiceless their own means of self-expression.

One of the first films to attempt such restructuring was *Daquilema*, a short film of 28 minutes made in 1982. Based on a script written by Marcelo Cevallos, this short film reenacted the Indian uprisings that had occurred during the García Moreno dictatorship of the later nineteenth century in the province of Chimborazo. Daquilema was an Indian leader who urged his followers to rebel against the landowners. His valor and example encouraged various Indian communities to proclaim him their king. The reaction from the authorities and feudal lords was immediate—massive killings and the public execution of Daquilema. Besides having won awards for best script, best actor, and best music, *Daquilema* impressed viewers for having allowed modern-day Indians to portray themselves (i.e., their ancestors) in the re-creation of their own story.

Don Eloy, another short film produced in 1982, also experimented with techniques and strategies designed to create a work of historical authenticity and shared authorship. Under the direction of Camilo Luzuriaga, one of Ecuador's leading filmmakers, this documentary dealt with the life of Eloy Alfaro, Ecuador's revolutionary leader of 1895 who served as president during the early twentieth century. By displaying on screen authentic documents from the period and by recording testimonies from the common people of the times, Luzuriaga reconstructed the Liberal Revolution and Alfaro's deeds. Rather than depend exclusively on modern actors and movie props to re-interpret and/or re-create the past, he elaborated a pastiche in which interviews, photographs, testimonies, and re-creations of scenes from the past moved modern viewers closer to the film's subject.

In *Quito, país de la mitad* (Quito, Country of the Middle), a third documentary made in 1982, its director, José Corral, utilized many of the techniques found in *Daquilema* and *Don Eloy*. Winner of an award for best photography, the film examined the remote origins of the indigenous population of Pichincha province and its capital city of Quito. With a commitment to being as accurate as possible in his depiction of the film's subjects, Corral combined pertinent historical documents with photographs of important archaeological sites and of the region's flora and fauna. Furthermore, the film presented some of the Indians' ceremonies, traditions, and celebrations that were still being practiced. The most important and groundbreaking innovation, however, was the use of the Indian language, *Quichua*, for the documentary's narration. The choice of language was Corral's way of reaffirming the legitimacy of his subjects' authorial voice. Any other language would have offered viewers a mere translation of a culture that continues to create and express itself.

Gustavo and Igor Guayasamín, two of Ecuador's most prominent filmmakers, have devoted significant time and effort to portraying the country's Indians on screen. Much of their work is the fruit of years of living and interacting with their Indian subjects. *Los hieleros del Chimborazo* (The Icemakers from Chimborazo), which Gustavo directed in 1981, has become a classic documentary in the testimonial vein. Winner of first prize in a film competition in Huelva, Spain (1981) and second prize in a documentary film festival in Moscow (1982), *Los hieleros del Chimborazo* follows the daily struggle of the Indians who gather ice from the region's high mountaintops and then transport it to village markets. Every minute of the film captures the Indians' ability to overcome the high altitudes and freezing temperatures of the Andes. Notwithstanding the editorial process of filmmaking, Gustavo Guayasamín avoids staging or reinventing his material; instead, his use of the camera empowers the icemakers to take charge of their own compelling story.

In 1988, the Guayasamín brothers collaborated to film the documentary *Tiag: Lo inagotable* (Tiag: The Inexhaustible). The piece offers audiences a broad view of life in an Indian community. In a spontaneous collage of multiple sequences presented with no fixed chronological order and without a script, the Guayasamíns offer live scenes of harrowing, grazing, planting, and celebrating religious ceremonies. *Tiag* is a comprehensive testimonial about a community at work and at play (Larrea, "Tiag" 53). Of special importance is the film's depiction of how the community combines Western and indigenous religious practices. By juxtaposing a Catholic bishop's call for the pope to ordain more Indian priests with a local shaman who performs a ceremony, the Guayasamíns capture the profoundly syncretic nature of Christianity among Ecuador's indigenous communities (Larrea, "Tiag" 54).

Mónica Vásquez is another outstanding filmmaker who has brought international distinction to Ecuador's cinema. Her most acclaimed documentary to date is *Tiempo de mujeres* (Women's Time), which she completed in 1987. The film is about the small community of Santa Rosa, which is near Cuenca in Ecuador's southern highlands. Because of life's difficulties, the men of Santa Rosa left their families and traveled to Chicago and New York in search of jobs and financial security. Like many other emigrants, these men left

Ecuador with the expectation of eventually returning home with sufficient resources to begin a new life. In the meantime, however, Santa Rosa had become a community of women who had to learn to fend for themselves. It was this unique circumstance that attracted Vásquez.

Tiempo de mujeres follows Santa Rosa's women as they join together to re-create their community. Many of the traditions characteristic of patriarchal societies make it easy to appreciate the indomitable spirit that Vásquez captures in her documentary. Alone and unprepared, these women are left behind with debts, with plows and seeds for tilling the land, and with all of the physical labor required for a successful harvest ("Tiempo de mujeres" 66). Santa Rosa's women manage to survive and conserve what is theirs. Through assumption of unconventional roles and responsibilities, their story proves to be a powerful statement about the rightful place of women in Ecuadorian society.

Tiempo de mujeres and the other documentaries discussed above are representative of the best work that is being done in Ecuadorian film. Together they constitute a film genre that has provided audiences with alternative ways of understanding Ecuador's past and present. Just as writers and painters have dedicated their art to shaking up Ecuador's social order, so documentary filmmakers have learned to use their medium as a form of public service. It is clear that artistic expression in Ecuador is rarely self-indulgent; in most cases, it is understood that outstanding art must necessarily contribute to social change. The documentary films made since 1980 in Ecuador confirm that imperative.

Feature Films

The lack of resources and facilities has made it difficult for Ecuadorian cinema to develop a viable tradition of feature films. Ecuador's first feature-length talkie was not made until 1949. *Se conocieron en Guayaquil* (They Met in Guayaquil) was directed by Paco Villar, who collaborated with Ecuador Sono Films, a recently formed production company. In 1950, this same company produced a second feature film of fiction, *Amanecer en el Pichincha* (Dawn in Pichincha). *Se conocieron en Guayaquil* was the only Ecuadorian film listed in Georges Sadoul's *History of World Cinema*, which was published in 1967 (Vásquez et al. 26).

The little progress achieved in the production of feature films during the last two decades of the twentieth century has been due partly to the growth of television in Ecuador. Several made-for-television movies have been quite successful, especially the adaptations of two of Ecuador's most famous novels,

Cumandá and *El chulla Romero y Flores.* Television means more visibility and greater access to a broad viewing public. Nevertheless, Ecuadorian filmmakers cannot compete with imported feature films. Without an adequate infrastructure for distribution and promotion, filmmaking will never constitute a viable career in Ecuador.

As is so often the case, however, every rule has its exception. Notwithstanding the bleak prospects for feature films in Ecuador, Camilo Luzuriaga has established himself as Ecuador's premier moviemaker. Much of his training and development as a filmmaker can be traced to his participation in many of the film-related activities of the 1960s and 1970s that were designed to cultivate a new cinema and a more informed viewing audience. His first films belonged to the documentary genre and were highly didactic; *Don Eloy* (1982) is indicative of Luzuriaga's initial efforts.

In retrospect, however, one could argue that Luzuriaga was preparing the way for more ambitious film projects as early as 1982. His coproduction with Jorge Vivanco of *Chacón maravilla* (Chacón the Marvel) is a case in point. This 22-minute piece is about a shoeshine boy who befriends a wealthy young girl in need of companionship and understanding. Poor and a product of the city streets, Chacón uses fantasy to cope with life's struggles. The tall cement walls that enclose Alicia's spacious home symbolize a highly protected and isolated world that prevents her from growing emotionally and socially. Chacón gives Alicia the gift of imagination that promises to liberate her (*Catálogo de difusión* 120).

The way Luzuriaga and Vivanco combine fiction and social commentary in *Chacón maravilla* is noteworthy. The filmmakers demonstrate that a child's fantasies do not exist in a social vacuum. Through the innocence of childhood, the audience discovers how people of different social classes and backgrounds need each other in relationships that are not exploitative. Although the film's message is never overbearing, it challenges viewers to rethink Ecuador's social order. *Chacón maravilla* strikes a balance between a cinema that is entertainment and one that is a medium for social change.

In 1990, Luzuriaga produced one of his most ambitious films. *La tigra* (The Tigress) was a feature film based on a short story written by Ecuador's José de la Cuadra in 1935. It was no coincidence that Luzuriaga chose a story that was written during the height of Latin America's literary period of social realism. Just as he and other young filmmakers had been experimenting with ways to make films both artistically and socially responsible, so the writers of the 1930s had devoted themselves to the same mission.

Basically, *La tigra* is a story about three sisters who live in the countryside of the Coast. Their parents are murdered by a group of intruders. The oldest sister, Francisca, witnesses the tragedy from a hiding place and kills the five burglars with her father's shotgun. From that night on, everyone calls Francisca the Tigress. As the result of her parents' death, she becomes the absolute mistress of the family's property.

The trauma of the crime moves Francisca to take vengeance against all men. Her vengeance is carried out by becoming sexually liberated; with the power derived from being a feudal landowner, she is able to dominate all of the men with whom she has contact. In effect, all the power of the region is in her hands, and because of the propensity for mythmaking among rural peoples, Francisca becomes larger than life.

This plot is merely the setting for a complex portrayal of rural Ecuador at a time when tradition and modernity were on a collision course. The original story pitted the countryside against the city, rural superstitions against urban forms of material progress, and one version of "truth" against another, especially with regard to women and their place in society. Above all, José de la Cuadra's objective was to interpret Ecuador's social history through the experiences of the common folk. Consequently, the story's descriptions and overall narration are not unlike the testimonial documentary, in which the filmmaker attempted to draw his audience closer to many of Ecuador's untold stories.

Recalling Luzuriaga's experience as a documentary filmmaker, one can understand his attraction to *La tigra*. By adapting the literary text to the big screen, Luzuriaga was able to revisit a time, place, and culture that had become far removed from his contemporary viewers and their respective experiences. Although Luzuriaga's depiction of Francisca as the embodiment of nature's primeval forces might be objectionable to some, it is clear that the film's technical innovations and camera work represent a giant step forward in the creation of a vibrant and vital national cinema.

CONCLUSION

There is no doubt that Ecuador has enough talented people to sustain a cinema of high quality and broad public interest. Limited public exposure should not suggest the absence of an Ecuadorian cinema. Much has been accomplished during the twentieth century despite the obvious lack of financial support and the overwhelming competition from United States movies that continue to flood the Ecuadorian market. Until the country reaches some basic level of economic security, however, it is more than probable that Ecuador's moviemakers will produce primarily documentaries and short films for alternative audiences.

REFERENCES

Burton, Julianne. *Cinema and Social Change in Latin America: Conversations with Filmmakers*. Austin: University of Texas Press, 1986.

Catálogo de difusión. Quito: Editorial Casa de la Cultura Ecuatoriana, 1994.

"La cinematografía nacional." *Palabra Suelta*, 2 (1987), 65.

Granda Noboa, Wilma. *Cine silente en Ecuador: 1895–1935*. Quito: Editorial Casa de la Cultura Ecuatoriana, 1995.

Larrea, Ramiro. "Perspectivas de un cine popular en el Ecuador." *Palabra Suelta*, 3 (1987), 52.

———. "Tiag: Autenticidad y mimetismo." *Palabra suelta*, 4 (1988), 53–54.

Muñoz Martineaux, Ronnie. "Surgimiento de un verdadero cine nacional." *Espejo*, 4, no. 5 (May 1982), 37–42.

Saltos G., Napoleón, and Lola Vázquez, eds. *Ecuador: Su realidad*. 5th ed. Quito: Fundación "José Peralta," 1997.

"Tiempo de mujeres." *Palabra Suelta*, 2 (1987), 66.

Vásquez, Teresa, Mercedes Serrano, Patricia Gudiño, and Wilma Granda, comps. *Cronología de la cultura cinematográfica: 1849–1986*. Quito: Editorial Casa de la Cultura Ecuatoriana, 1987.

6

Literature

Ecuadorian writers have often lamented that publishing their work in Ecuador is tantamount to remaining unpublished. This claim brings to light numerous issues that profoundly affect the reading public's perception of Ecuadorian writers and their artistic value. Unfortunately, few readers know much about Ecuadorian literature because it has not been readily accessible; consequently, there is the erroneous assumption that Ecuador has not contributed significantly to Latin American literature.

Unlike Mexico and Argentina, two of Latin America's larger and wealthier countries, Ecuador has never developed a publishing infrastructure capable of producing, promoting, and distributing its literature on a broad basis. Within the country, editions rarely exceed 1,000 copies, and it is still common for writers to leave their works on consignment at local bookstores. Moreover, in Ecuador books seldom reach readers who do not live in the cities where they are printed. Thus, accessibility not only has affected the international reading public's perception of Ecuadorian literature, but also continues to limit the extent to which Ecuadorians are knowledgeable about their own writers.

The inadequacies of the publishing system in Ecuador are intimately linked to a small reading public that still renders unlikely most attempts to earn a living from writing/publishing/selling books. Illiteracy and poverty partly explain the problem. The government and private sectors are reluctant to invest limited resources in cultural projects that are supposedly destined for an elite minority (highly literate individuals with the wherewithal and desire to purchase expensive books).

Today's writers in Ecuador are clearly conditioned by the paradox of working in a nation that is both Third World and postmodern. On the one hand, the abject poverty of millions brings into question the need for literature; on the other hand, an economy driven by consumerism and a growing interest in cyberspace has mesmerized many potential readers with CD-ROMs and state-of-the-art satellite dishes. As a result, bookstores and publishing houses have little interest in literature per se. A brief visit to Guayaquil, Ecuador's largest city, with over 2 million residents, is illustrative of this situation. Beyond the shops that specialize in school supplies or in costly hardbound editions of encyclopedias and technology-related books, there is no major bookstore interested in promoting works by Ecuadorian authors.

In addition to their limited appeal to the national mainstream, Ecuadorian writers are even further removed from foreign readers, especially from those who depend on translations. With very few exceptions, there is no viable market for Ecuadorian books outside Ecuador, and consequently few people see past Ecuador's stereotype—a small country that has little more than bananas or coffee to offer people who live beyond its borders.

Despite these bleak conditions, Ecuador does have a rich tradition of writers and outstanding literature. The purpose of this chapter is to uncover the artistic merit and the social importance of Ecuadorian letters. In view of just how financially fruitless writing and publishing are in Ecuador, there must be a profound appreciation for those writers (and readers) who have been relentless in their efforts to create an alternative space for a different Ecuador, for an Ecuador that transcends the extremes of widespread poverty and unbridled consumerism.

THE HOUSE OF ECUADORIAN CULTURE

Before discussing some of Ecuador's principal writers and literary works, it is important to note briefly a few of the strategies that intellectuals have employed, especially in the twentieth century, to ensure the development and growth of the country's literature. In the absence of firm governmental policies dealing specifically with cultural activities outside of the country's formal system of education, Benjamín Carrión led a successful effort in 1944 to create the Casa de la Cultura Ecuatoriana (House of Ecuadorian Culture), a semiautonomous institution that would receive governmental subsidies and be in charge of promoting cultural expression. With regard to literature, the Casa constituted an immediate catalyst, particularly with the creation of its own publication center. Carrión was committed to the production and distribution of Ecuador's literature.

Although the Casa has had a history of controversy and conflict due to internal disputes, questionable accounting procedures, unpopular editorial decisions, inadequate funding, and a leadership that too often has been both uninspired and uninspiring, the institution has survived for more than half a century. Its many publications, exhibits, symposia, and library loan programs that have taken books in vans to underserved areas throughout the country are testimony that the Casa has succeeded in establishing a continuous presence for literature in a society that still struggles to provide most of its citizens with food, shelter, and jobs.

As an institution officially recognized by the government, the Casa has gained some leverage to challenge long-standing prejudices that would deny artists and writers a central place in Ecuadorian society. With its headquarters in Quito and branches located in most of the country's 20 provinces, the Casa has inspired a stream of diverse groups from both the private and the public sectors to sponsor literary journals, collections of Ecuadorian classics, literary histories, and anthologies of literatures from throughout the world. Although many of these projects have been short-lived, flourishing during economic booms and disappearing with diminishing banana and oil profits, they are a reminder that literary production has been a constant in Ecuadorian society since long before the Casa's founding in 1944. Indeed, each project belongs to a broader continuum that can be traced back to the latter part of the eighteenth century.

The importance of the Casa de la Cultura Ecuatoriana should not be underestimated. Despite fiscal obstacles and frequent skepticism, the institution has kept alive the notion that cultural policies ought to be an integral part of modern Ecuador's social and political agenda. Moreover, Casa-sponsored activities and accomplishments through the years debunk such myths as the isolated artist and the detached writer. Literature and its practitioners have played a vital role in Ecuadorian history, and the Casa represents the embodiment of such a legacy.

EUGENIO ESPEJO AND THE BEGINNINGS OF A NATIONAL LITERATURE

Benjamín Carrión frequently emphasized that the Casa de la Cultura Ecuatoriana was unlike any other cultural institution. Whereas museums, literary societies, and scientific academies were traditionally intended for a small elite of wealthy and highly educated citizens, Ecuador's House of Culture claimed to belong to all Ecuadorians. Not only did the unpretentious word Casa symbolize the institution's commitment to creating a common meeting ground for the nation's diverse social classes, but it also alluded to a democratic project that would make the arts and sciences increasingly accessible to the majority of Ecuadorians.

Though much controversy surrounds whether or not the Casa has actually achieved democratization, what is most interesting is the extent to which Ecuador's cultural history, and in particular its literature, continues to be so politically charged. Because illiteracy has been so pervasive throughout Ecuadorian history, the ability to read and write has frequently been a source of power and privilege controlled by a small group of Ecuadorians. With the gradual increase in literacy, however, Ecuadorian literature slowly became a virtual battleground where writers from socially diverse backgrounds championed conflicting causes and ideologies. Without abandoning literature's aesthetic traditions, Ecuador's most accomplished writers have struggled to create a literature that is both artistically pleasing and socially responsible. Although that balance has frequently proven to be elusive, Ecuadorian literature has evolved as a unique account of the nation's never-ending struggle to define itself.

One of the first writers to lay the foundation for a national literature was Eugenio Espejo (1747–1795). As a product of the Enlightenment, he was convinced that empirical and scientific knowledge was essential if one hoped to discover truth and happiness. Under Spanish rule, however, the prevailing philosophy was rooted in the Counter-Reformation and Scholasticism, which emphasized absolute acceptance of established authority. Espejo rejected Spanish thought and politics, and became a precursor of Ecuadorian independence. Most noteworthy was his decision to voice his opposition through literature, particularly through the essay. By consciously employing literature as a means of social protest, Espejo attacked the ruling class's penchant for a literature imbued with ceremonial conceits and flawed imitations of Spanish baroque literature. In short, Espejo's rebellion against Spanish obscurantism and authoritarianism was intimately linked to his rejection of the period's dominant literary canon.

Espejo protested against Spain (and against everything Spanish) because he was deeply aware of a new identity that was taking shape in America, in Ecuador, and even in himself. Despite Spain's insistence that its colonies were Spanish, and although many creoles (people of Spanish blood born in America) felt a strong allegiance to their European roots, the many disparities inherent in the colonial institutions (e.g., the government, the church, and the military) made it painfully clear that Americans were not equal to Spaniards. Espejo understood the distinction and suffered the consequences in more ways than one. Although he was a medical doctor and a lawyer, a member of the educated elite, he was also a mestizo, whose father was an Indian and whose mother was a mulatto. In effect, his heritage and ancestry were suspect, and the emotional conflict so apparent in his decision to deny his real surname (Chushig) suggests the beginnings of an identity crisis that, paradoxically, became a cultural and psychological blueprint for future Ecuadorians.

As a writer, Espejo was a satirist and polemicist. In 1779, he began to circulate his *Nuevo Luciano* (New Lucian), a collection of nine critical dialogues modeled after those of the Greek humorist Lucian. Espejo attacked the educational system in Quito for being unduly harsh, pedantic, obtuse, and irrelevant. In his *Reflexiones* (Reflections), dated 1785, Espejo discussed effective ways to combat the smallpox virus that had recently ravaged many Indian communities in Ecuador. His observations about hygiene and medical care were revolutionary for his time and, most important, they constituted an open attack against many of the superstitions and old wives' tales that dominated the medical practice of the period.

In 1792, Espejo launched his principal contribution to Ecuadorian literature and culture. *Primicias de la cultura de Quito* (The First Fruits of Culture from Quito) was Ecuador's first newspaper, and although Espejo managed to publish only seven issues, his efforts would mark a new direction for future writers. Espejo understood the need to reach a larger audience, one that had little patience with dense writing but hungered for new ideas and honest information. *Primicias* was Espejo's most revolutionary work, both in content and in accessibility. He criticized church authorities and Spanish loyalists; at the same time, he informed his readers about events taking place in the rest of America. In short, Espejo used the newspaper as a clarion for independence. Consequently, Spanish authorities persecuted and imprisoned him. Although Espejo died in prison, his revolutionary message and example greatly influenced those leaders who in 1809 initiated the armed struggle for political independence.

Espejo has come to represent an intellectual prototype for Ecuador and the rest of Latin America. He was a highly educated mestizo who spent his entire life trying to reconcile the contradictions of colonialism. While Espejo yearned for acceptance from his European counterparts, the latter refused to forgive his racial impurities. Thus, Espejo found himself torn between two conflicting worlds. Like so many intellectuals of later generations who belong to a growing multicultural middle class, Espejo struggled to forge a new identity that would be true to both his European training and his native origins.

Nineteenth-Century Writers and National Consolidation

Espejo was a transitional figure in Ecuadorian history. His intellectual curiosity and his confidence in scientific observation as the basis for objective truth were the product of the neoclassical and encyclopedic mentality of the eighteenth century. At the same time, Espejo's passionate defiance of the status quo revealed a spirit that would characterize much of nineteenth-century romanticism and nationalism in Ecuador and the rest of Latin America.

By the 1820s, when most Latin American countries had gained independence, intellectuals found themselves engrossed in defining their respective countries. The birth of new nations required new constitutions and a new sense of national identity. Such was the state of affairs in Ecuador; intellectuals had set about the task of formalizing what Espejo had intuited a generation earlier. Whereas Espejo had focused his efforts on destroying a Spanish system that was intrusive and unjust, the new intellectuals had to construct a new world order from the ashes left by the Wars of Independence.

José Joaquín Olmedo (1780–1847)

José Joaquín Olmedo, a poet and diplomat, was one of Ecuador's first nation builders. His work thus exemplifies the close relationship that has long existed between literature and politics in Latin America. Aside from serving in numerous governmental posts, Olmedo earned his place in history primarily for having written the most memorable poem ever published about Simón Bolívar, the liberator of much of South America.

La victoria de Junín: Canto a Bolívar (The Victory at Junín: Song to Bolívar) consists of 900 verses and was completed in 1825, shortly after Bolívar's definitive victories against the Spanish royalist forces in 1824. True to his classical education, Olmedo incorporated into his *Canto* numerous features that he had learned from reading the ancient Roman poets Horace and Virgil. In fact, critics have pointed out that the poem's initial stanza is an imitation of the fifth ode of Book III of Horace.

The classical forms that Olmedo borrowed should not suggest, however, a lack of originality. Unlike the controlled style and moderate tone typical of classical and neoclassical works, the *Canto* is specifically about America, and it explodes with hyperbole and unrestrained enthusiasm for Bolívar and his liberating armies. In fact, Bolívar criticized Olmedo for being excessively passionate in his battle descriptions. Olmedo understood, however, that heroic poetry as a literary form was totally consistent with a nationalist project that would define the newborn nations, in part, through their heroes. Bolívar was (and still is) a source of pride for all America; his courage and victories symbolized a Latin America that was destined to be triumphant. *Canto a Bolívar* was therefore exuberant; Bolívar's glory was everyone's glory.

The extent to which Olmedo intended *Canto a Bolívar* to be read as a Latin American manifesto, or as an affirmation of a new cultural identity totally different from European models, becomes patently clear with the sudden appearance of Huayna Capac, the last Inca to rule over a unified empire untouched by Spanish conquerors. Although many readers have criticized the Inca's presence as intrusive and far-fetched, many others have praised Olmedo for honoring Latin America's Indian heritage at such a defining moment in its history.

As a rhetorical device, Huayna Capac enabled Olmedo to address several concerns. First, because the Inca denounces Spanish cruelty against the Indians, Olmedo was able to remind readers that their struggle for independence had been a moral imperative. Second, because the grandiose portrait of the Inca stood in stark contrast to the suffering Indians of the nineteenth century, Olmedo could counter any tendency of Latin Americans to be ashamed of their Indian heritage. Third, because Huayna Capac was a reminder of past unity and harmony, Olmedo used the Inca to "exhort Bolívar to maintain the unity among the peoples who fought for Independence, and to establish just laws to govern the recently liberated continent" (Harrison, *Entre el tronar épico* . . . 56; author's translation).

Despite his intentions, Olmedo did not create a meaningful connection between his readers and the Indians. For many of Olmedo's contemporaries and their descendants, who believed they mirrored the best of European culture, Huayna Capac and the Inca past were too remote and too exotic to be accepted as an integral part of the modern Latin American experience. Consequently, the wise and judicious Huayna Capac could be little more than a pre-Columbian symbol, a convenient figure to protest Spanish greed and cruelty. As for the real Indians, their deprivation and non-European ways continued to be repulsive. Frequently, they were an excuse used to explain Latin America's inability to compete with Europe and the United States.

The Indians' controversial place in literature and society would become a central theme in Ecuadorian history. Olmedo had defined the parameters of the debate: Indians as heroes or as victims, as a source of national pride or of national shame. By the middle of the nineteenth century, when writers consciously worked at creating a national literature, the Indian presence would occupy center stage, particularly in the works of Juan León Mera, one of Ecuador's giants of nineteenth-century romanticism.

Juan León Mera (1832–1894)

With political independence secured, the new nations undertook the task of distinguishing themselves from each other. For Ecuador, a country that had been part of both Peru and Colombia at different times during the colonial period, the challenge was daunting. To complicate matters even more, Ecuador's first president was Juan José Flores, one of Bolívar's Venezuelan generals. Because its physical and cultural borders were so often in flux, and because the country's name did not exist before 1830, Ecuador's national project seemed to be adrift. Political disorder, regional rivalries, and mixed loyalties created an environment of chaos. Even though each interest group promoted its agenda as an authentic expression of patriotism and nationalism, such sentiments were still more illusory than real.

Writers were not aloof from the political battles that were being fought in Ecuadorian society. They, too, were involved in building a nation. Like Olmedo, who was a poet and a statesman, many carried out numerous functions simultaneously. Others viewed literature as an effective means to promote a particular social and political agenda. Indeed, the distinctions between writing and governing were often blurred. Nevertheless, as a general principle, one can posit that while politicians openly sought power and influence to impose their national views, writers used literature to create a national portrait that would determine how Ecuadorians would define themselves individually and collectively.

Juan León Mera is a prime example of a writer whose literary contributions were an integral part of those early efforts to forge a sense of nation and unity among Ecuadorians. He wrote Ecuador's national anthem and, true to the prevailing romanticism of the period, he became a collector of legends and folklore that supposedly embodied Ecuador's uniqueness among nations. His critical history of Ecuadorian poetry, *Ojeada histórico-crítica sobre la poesía ecuatoriana* (1868), was a landmark anthology that brought together three centuries of previously sporadic and disconnected poetry, and established a sense of continuity that would be the basis for future histories of Ecuador's national literature.

For Mera, Ecuador was Hispanic, mestizo, and Catholic. He was a political conservative who believed the period's turmoil and unrest could be countered by acknowledging common symbols and values. Thus, one language and one religion were paramount to any national project that sought order and unity. Ecuador, however, was never as one-dimensional and homogeneous as Mera had proposed. For the most part, the large Indian population did not speak Spanish, and their religious practices retained much from pre-Columbian times.

Curiously enough, Mera was very knowledgeable of that Indian past. In fact, he was among the first to call for a serious study of Quichua, one of the principal languages spoken by Ecuadorian Indians. Moreover, a significant portion of his literary writings contain numerous *quichuismos* (words and phrases taken from Quichua) that Ecuadorian speakers of Spanish had assimilated into their daily speech.

Mera's interest in Ecuador's Indians was consistent with his concept of the mestizo nation. The Indians and their customs gave Ecuador a uniqueness that distinguished it from other countries. Unfortunately, that uniqueness was rarely more than a reference to the national landscape; the Indians were simply a part of Ecuador's flora and fauna. As far as being accepted as people, Mera and his readers did not consider Indians to be their equals; at best, Indians were "noble savages" to be assimilated into a civilized nation that was Spanish-speaking and Catholic. Thus, a mestizo Ecuador referred to a process of "whitening" or "Westernizing" rather than to a democratic project anchored in tolerance and respect for cultural differences.

Mera's ambivalent and controversial position regarding the Indians and their place in the nation is clearly evident in his novel *Cumandá*. Published in 1879, *Cumandá* has long been considered one of Latin America's classic romantic novels; many readers have compared it to François Chateaubriand's *Atalá*. Cumandá is a beautiful Indian maiden from Ecuador's Amazonian region who falls in love with Carlos, an aspiring poet and son of a wealthy landowner from Ecuador's ruling class. After Carlos's father loses his infant daughter and wife in a fire that was part of an Indian uprising, he decides to become a missionary priest as an act of penitence for his previous cruelty to his Indian servants. The church assigns him to a remote village in the Amazon; Carlos accompanies him. Carlos wanders about aimlessly; the jungle terrain, untouched by so-called civilization, heightens his poetic sensibilities.

According to romantic formulas of the nineteenth century, young lovers from two different worlds generally suffer tragedy and broken hearts. In the case of Cumandá and Carlos, their impossible love is doomed from the moment they fall in love. Cumandá is Carlos's sister, who as an infant supposedly had perished in the fire, but actually had been rescued by an Indian woman and raised as her daughter.

Although the novel's story might seem contrived, *Cumandá* is a tour de force of literary Americanism, romanticism, and Ecuadorian nationalism. Indeed, more than a mere piece of fiction, Mera's novel constitutes a social document that is indispensable to understanding the dominant values and mind-set that characterized nineteenth-century Ecuador and helped consolidate the nation's official image of itself.

From the opening pages of the novel, Mera addresses a European audience and celebrates his work's physical setting as pure and pristine. Unlike the rest of the civilized world, the Amazon is a piece of Eden with unbounded fertility and open spaces that symbolize all of Latin America as a promised land of future greatness. Because many of the geographical descriptions of the Amazon region are accurate, Mera succeeds in blurring the line between fiction and reality. Latin America, that collection of newly born nations, did indeed have much to offer the rest of the world. Thus, the novel in no small measure was intended to gain the respect of Europeans, the guardians of civilization and masters of progress. For Mera and his contemporaries, such respect and acceptance were essential to legitimize Latin America's place in the civilized world.

"Civilization and barbarianism," a phrase coined in 1845 by Argentina's Domingo Sarmiento, has profoundly influenced the way many people perceive Latin America's place within the family of nations. The same dichotomy has been expressed in many ways: superior and inferior, developed and underdeveloped, powerful and powerless, First World and Third World. In each case, Latin America has been portrayed as the weaker of the pair.

There is no question that Mera's *Cumandá* is an integral part of that cultural debate. While his many references to Nature as a source of growth and development are a call for everyone to be optimistic about Latin America's future, the underlying assumption is that success will be achieved when the forces of civilization (Europe and the United States) overcome those of barbarianism (Latin America). The function of the Indians in *Cumandá* is to confirm the validity of such a formula.

Notwithstanding the numerous descriptions of Indian customs and cultural practices that make *Cumandá* a kind of ethnographic essay, Mera leaves no doubt among his readers that Indians are savages whose only means for salvation (spiritual and social) is their acceptance of Catholicism. Symbolically, much more is at issue than the Indians in Mera's response to the "civilization and barbarianism" debate. All of Latin America ought to emulate its European forebears.

Thus, Mera's direct appeal to his European readers was his way of demonstrating that, as an intellectual, he had been "civilized." Despite his mestizo background (certainly cultural if not also racial), he had been accepted as a corresponding member of Spain's Royal Academy of Language. Hispanism and Christianity had saved him (and other Latin Americans) in much the same way that he had proposed for the savage Indians in *Cumandá*. The nation had found its image in Mera's novel.

Juan Montalvo (1832–1889)

Juan Montalvo was Ecuador's other giant of romanticism and, arguably, the country's greatest writer. Unlike the conservative and Catholic Mera, who aspired to form a nation through conciliation and assimilation, Montalvo was a fiery liberal characterized by anticlericalism and combative political essays. In the tradition of Argentina's Domingo Sarmiento, Peru's Manuel González Prada and Cuba's José Martí, Montalvo exemplified the writer who utilized literature to combat dictators and despotism in general.

In 1866, Montalvo began publishing *El cosmopolita* (The Cosmopolitan), a politically inspired magazine in which he attacked Gabriel García Moreno, Ecuador's strong-willed dictator who ruled the country from 1861 to 1875. Montalvo confronted the government's abuses of power with a passionate defense of such basic freedoms as those of worship and association. Years of persecution and exile followed until García Moreno was assassinated. Upon learning of the dictator's death, Montalvo celebrated by claiming that his writings had killed García Moreno: "*Mi pluma lo mató*" (My pen killed him.).

Montalvo's career as a political polemicist did not end with García Moreno's death. Political turmoil and instability continued to plague Ecuador. Between 1880 and 1882, Montalvo published *Las catilinarias*, a biting attack against dictators in general, and the period's principal villain and strongman, Captain General José Ignacio de Veintemilla, in particular. *Las catilinarias* was a direct reference to Cicero and his four speeches written against the Roman conspirator Catiline. Like Cicero, Montalvo also denounced mediocre politicians in a rich and eloquent prose that many literary critics have considered to be exemplary writing.

Montalvo's exquisite prose style and deep appreciation for classical literary models are especially evident in his *Siete tratados* (Seven Treatises), published in 1882, and in *Los capítulos que se le olvidaron a Cervantes* (The Chapters Forgotten by Cervantes), which appeared posthumously in 1895. Each work is a collection of reflections on such eternal themes as beauty, virtue, morality, idealism, and heroism. The expansiveness of each theme enabled Montalvo to lose himself in a language rich with metaphors, literary allusions, and classical exempla; in each case, he reminded his readers that aesthetics and ethics were inseparable. He was convinced that a genuine appreciation for beauty would necessarily lead to virtuous behavior.

Despite the many ideological and artistic differences that separated Montalvo from Mera, he, too, was very much a product of the "civilization and barbarianism" debate. At the same time that he was denouncing Ecuador's political and social ills, Montalvo was able to distance himself from the local savagery by mastering the European classics. As an intellectual with a European education, Montalvo saw himself as proof that Ecuadorians had the ability to prosper and grow. Thus, his polemical and artistic writings reflected the prevailing mentality of the times: progress was dependent upon adopting European ways. Unfortunately, Montalvo did not seem to be aware of Eugenio Espejo's tragic fate some 100 years earlier. Despite being an accomplished scholar and physician, Espejo never earned full access to Europe's civilized world. Curiously, one of Montalvo's greatest disappointments was not being named a corresponding member of Spain's Royal Academy of Language.

Ecuador's original nation builders (and most others from the rest of Latin America) had not freed themselves from Europe's colonial dominance. Despite Bolívar's military victories at the beginning of the nineteenth century, Ecuador's intellectuals continued to emulate foreign models, a practice that distorted the national image. Although it would be a grave error to deny a European heritage in Ecuador (or in Latin America, in general), the intellectuals' fascination with Europe created an imbalance in their thinking. Colonialist prejudices led to self-deprecation; consequently, most solutions to problems expressed within the "civilization and barbarianism" paradigm were, in fact, a denial of anything non-European.

Not until the twentieth century would writers consciously reassess their sense of nation. The gradual rejection of nineteenth-century images that had defined the nation as a reflection of the values and cultural background of a small and privileged minority coincided with the emergence of middle-class writers who could not escape their multiracial and multiethnic heritage. Moreover, the Liberal Revolution of 1895 brought to Ecuadorian politics a growing concern for the majority of Ecuadorians, who had been denied social justice by the country's ruling elite. As the debate over the nation's problems broadened, Ecuador's new breed of writers allied themselves with the masses; together with Ecuador's exploited workers and people of color, the writers saw themselves as social outcasts who needed to challenge the nation's oligarchic traditions of privilege and power.

Notwithstanding the differences that separated the generations, Ecuador's principal writers of the nineteenth century did establish numerous traditions that continue to characterize Ecuadorian writers and their literary work. Olmedo combined literature and public service; Mera promoted an appreciation for Ecuador's indigenous cultures; Montalvo balanced his social and political agenda with artistry and eloquence. In each case, society and literature proved to be inseparable, demonstrating the extent to which writers have played a fundamental role in Ecuador's national history.

THE GENERATION OF 1930

Most literary historians refer to 1930 as the beginning of modern Ecuadorian literature. In that year, three young aspiring writers from Guayaquil joined efforts and published a collection of 24 short stories that would change the course of Ecuadorian literature. In *Los que se van: Cuentos del cholo i del montuvio* (Those Who Go Away: Stories About the Cholo and the Montuvio), Demetrio Aguilera Malta (1909–1981), Enrique Gil Gilbert (1912–1973), and Joaquín Gallegos Lara (1911–1947) broke with traditional Ecuadorian fiction by putting at center stage characters whose roots were among the country's masses living along the Pacific coast.[1] Unlike previous works that used the poor and the socially marginalized as superficial examples of local color and picturesque customs, *Los que se van* opened the way for Ecuadorians to examine the human tragedies that the country's exploited and forgotten masses had to endure. In a literary style that would be called social realism, the collection's stories depicted an array of coastal characters whose hardships, fears, ambitions, strengths, and weaknesses would contribute to a more democratic and inclusive national portrait.

It is not surprising that *Los que se van* provoked anger and condemnation among many readers. Unaccustomed to the crude language and vivid descriptions of poverty, squalor, and violence that characterized the stories, they considered the material offensive and, generally speaking, in bad taste. With few exceptions, the literature written until then had not focused on an Ecuador composed of mestizos and the poor. These characters traditionally provided readers with entertainment: they were the stereotypical buffoons, the happy masses whose ignorance and innocence were endearing, or the country bumpkins who frequently spoke an antiquated Spanish reminiscent of classical times.

With social realism, however, writers understood that frank treatment of Ecuador's masses was essential if they were to create an authentic literature, a literature that would be relevant to the national experience. Such relevance meant that literature had to be socially and politically engaged. The young writers had been deeply affected by the Mexican Revolution of 1910, the Russian Revolution of 1917, and the growing influence of socialist politics throughout the world. Thus, for literature to be responsive to a new social milieu, writers believed they had to be active agents of change.

Such commitment, however, did not mean a literature of propaganda rather than one of artistic expression. *Los que se van* was a revolutionary literary text because it challenged readers to see and imagine the world differently. New forms of characterization and innovative language were the principal means of subverting the prevailing social order. By drawing their protagonists from mestizo Ecuador instead of from the ruling elite, writers redefined the nation's hierarchical structure of human relationships. Through social realism, readers began to discover that they were inextricably bound to the misery and deprivation suffered by the majority of Ecuadorians.

After the publication of *Los que se van*, Ecuadorian literature became a kind of laboratory in which writers carried out two fundamental projects. First, they uncovered the many faces of exploitation and oppression that characterized Ecuador; second, they studied the customs and traditions of a people who previously had gone largely unnoticed and unappreciated. Clearly, social protest and an incipient form of cultural anthropology had become the principal traits of Ecuadorian literature.

Grupo de Guayaquil

José de la Cuadra (1903–1941) and Alfredo Pareja Diezcanseco (1908–1993) joined the authors of *Los que se van* to form the Grupo de Guayaquil. Together, these five writers dominated Ecuador's literary scene for several decades. Many of their works have become national classics. Among their most memorable works are Cuadra's *Los Sangurimas* (1934; The Sangurimas Family), Pareja Diezcanseco's *Baldomera* (1938), Aguilera Malta's *Don Goyo* (1933), Gallegos Lara's *Las cruces sobre el agua* (1946; Crosses on the Water), and Gil Gilbert's *Nuestro pan* (1942; Our Daily Bread).

The Grupo de Guayaquil worked diligently to offer readers a coherent literary project marked by specific guiding principles. The members met regularly to discuss their objectives as writers; they read and critiqued each other's works, and also studied the texts that each had received from other countries. Clearly, the group's collective efforts signaled the emergence of a new approach to writing in Ecuador. Unlike the isolated artist who cultivated his literary interests intuitively and as a kind of hobby, the Grupo de Guayaquil adopted a professional approach to literature. Together, they sought to master their craft as both readers and writers; they understood that outstanding and meaningful literature was the product of mastering its fundamental components (style, structure, tone, point of view, characterization). Such mastery required extensive study and continuous effort.

Although they shared a commitment to social realism and had a common perspective regarding their role as responsible writers, the Grupo de Guayaquil was not sectarian or homogeneous. Each member wrote about his concerns and obsessions in a unique and personal narrative style. Cuadra's fiction, for example, concentrated on the Coast's *montuvios*, whose rural traditions were undergoing dramatic changes with the advent of modernization. While Cuadra explored many of the *montuvios'* superstitions, customs, and conflicts, he utilized irony and ambiguity to capture the complexities surrounding Ecuador's impending social changes of the 1930s.

Cuadra's *Los Sangurimas* is a family saga that symbolizes the struggle between a feudal lifestyle and modernity. Nicasio Sangurimas holds absolute authority in his extended family, that has been created over several generations through violent boundary disputes, bloody feuds, and a total disregard for the legal rights of outsiders. Through force and fear, Nicasio has managed to create an image of invincibility and immortality; in fact, his power is so great that he becomes larger than life in the eyes of his subjects, who can no longer distinguish between the real Nicasio and the legendary one. Cuadra utilizes the gap between fiction and reality to defuse his character's power and, by association, the power of an anachronistic way of life that could no longer exist.

Cuadra's novel represents a pioneering effort in Latin American literature. Critics have called attention to the work's stylistic and thematic aspects that subsequent writers like Colombia's Nobel laureate, Gabriel García Márquez, developed in his *One Hundred Years of Solitude* (1967). In 1934, Cuadra employed irony and hyperbole (e.g., Nicasio's physical and sexual prowess) to blur the boundaries between objective and imagined reality. Moreover, Cuadra understood that the cultural clash between rural and urban Ecuador was due in large part to a similar kind of confusion. The constant migrations between regions by people who did not abandon entirely their previous lifestyles often made it difficult to distinguish between modernity and a feudal past. In other words, just as the forces of modernity were disrupting much of Ecuador's rural way of life, so were the vestiges of feudalism affecting the nation's urban centers. Consequently, whether he used literature to portray the Sangurimas family or the Ecuadorian nation, Cuadra did not express himself in simplistic dichotomies. Instead, he interpreted Ecuador's conflicts by emphasizing the social and cultural fluidity of the times.

Demetrio Aguilera Malta was another member of the Grupo de Guayaquil;

his novel, *Don Goyo* (1933), signaled major literary changes in both Ecuadorian and Latin American fiction. Like Cuadra, Aguilera Malta was enormously concerned with the effects of modernization on Ecuador's coastal communities, and in that respect, *Don Goyo* was consistent with many of the narrative works published throughout Latin America in the 1920s and 1930s. Often referred to as *novelas de la tierra* (novels of the land), these works had two overarching objectives: first, they argued that Latin America's cultural authenticity and uniqueness were to be found among its rural peoples; second, they denounced the period's capitalist growth and accelerated urbanization as threats to Latin America's native roots and identity.

In *Don Goyo*, Aguilera Malta focused on a community of *cholos* (mestizo coastal dwellers) who live on an island of mangroves near Guayaquil, the nation's principal seaport. The community's patriarchal leader, Don Goyo, evokes the harmonious relationship that ought to exist between man and nature. He understands nature's secrets, and through that knowledge, he emerges as a hero of epic and mythical proportions. Because Don Goyo is an integral part of his natural surroundings, which frequently assume human qualities, he is able to converse directly with nature. That kind of communication alternates between being an expression of erotic love and of sacred reverence.

To be sure, Aguilera Malta wrote his novel to denounce the destruction of Don Goyo's way of life by a capitalist economy that valued nature only as a source of financial gain. The novel's lasting value, however, has had more to do with its stylistic and thematic innovations than with the protest. Specifically, through numerous metaphors and images, Aguilera Malta creates the illusion that Don Goyo and the mangrove trees are an integral whole, without physical or temporal boundaries between them. The successful fusion of the vegetative and human worlds in *Don Goyo* established Aguilera Malta as a forerunner of magical realism in Latin American fiction.

It is clear that by juxtaposing the magical and the real, Aguilera Malta recreated the fluidity between diverse cultures and lifestyles that Cuadra captured in his fiction. Latin America's magical realism is not to be confused with Europe's surrealism or with its literature of the fantastic. While the latter are products of an author's imagination, magical realism has a historical and social foundation that challenges Western logic and experience. Aguilera Malta was acutely aware of the coexistence of chronological and mythical time among numerous communities in his social and cultural milieu of the 1930s. Thus, Don Goyo is much more than a voice of social protest against capitalist intrusions; he is a patriarch who embodies a remote and complex past that is struggling to survive as a legitimate way of life in modern Ecuador.

A key aspect of Aguilera Malta's holistic interpretation of Ecuadorian (and Latin American) society is his symbiotic view of nature and man. Unlike the prevailing notions that nature is either a threat to man which needs to be mastered or a source of wealth which needs to be exploited, Aguilera Malta argues for an ecological system that emphasizes cooperation rather than conflict. Long before the emergence of organized ecological movements to preserve the natural environment, Aguilera Malta understood that the destruction of nature would necessarily lead to man's self-destruction, in terms of both his physical and his cultural well-being. In this regard, "Don Goyo realizes that his fate is tied to that of the island milieu. His struggle is not with the tropical forest, but with outsiders who lack the knowledge and proper attitude to co-exist with it and who can only destroy the forest in a vain effort to make it render a profit" (Waag 74).

Although the other members of the Grupo de Guayaquil did not extensively explore the cultural and mythical dimensions of Ecuadorian society and its conflicts, they were just as influential as Cuadra and Aguilera Malta in the development of Ecuadorian fiction. Gallegos Lara and Pareja Diezcanseco devoted their works to interpreting life in Guayaquil, the Coast's major urban center. Their characters came from the city's masses, many of whom had migrated from the countryside in search of better opportunities, only to find poverty and frustration. Without abandoning their commitment to writing a literature of social protest, Gallegos Lara and Pareja Diezcanseco created some of Ecuadorian literature's most memorable characters, especially Alfredo Baldeón (*Las cruces sobre el agua*) and Baldomera (*Baldomera*). Gil Gilbert's *Nuestro pan* focused on the trials and tribulations of the Coast's rice growers. Rather than create a single dominant character, he told his story through the experiences of a collective protagonist, a community whose saga traced some fifty years of Ecuadorian history. In 1941, *Nuestro pan* won second prize in the Farrar Rinehart Publishing Company's prestigious competition for best Latin American novel.

Jorge Icaza, *Indigenismo*, and the Defense of Ecuador's Indians

During the same period that the Grupo de Guayaquil was creating a national literature populated mainly by the Coast's *montuvios* and *cholos*, writers from the Sierra, or Andean highlands, turned their attention to Ecuador's Indians. Unlike Olmedo and Mera, whose nineteenth-century works portrayed the nation's Indians as either heroes or noble savages, the social realists of the 1930s depicted their Indian characters as victims of exploitation and injustice. Whereas the earlier works were examples of *indianismo* and belonged to the larger corpus of romantic literature, the modern texts were an expression of *indigenismo*, a broadly conceived social and political movement that defended the human rights of Indians throughout Latin America.

Jorge Icaza (1906–1978) continues to be the country's foremost *indigenista* novelist of the twentieth century, and his *Huasipungo* (1934; *The Villagers*, 1964) is without doubt the most widely read novel written by an Ecuadorian. Basically, *Huasipungo* is a story about Alfonso Pereira, a powerful landowner whose good fortune is turning sour because of a financial crisis and an unwed pregnant daughter. Unable to repay a debt to his uncle, and fearful of the public scandal that his daughter's situation will cause among his high-society friends, Alfonso agrees to sell a large piece of his property to a group of investors from the United States who are interested in lumber and possible oil reserves. Before the lucrative transaction can occur, however, Alfonso must go to his estate and have his Indian servants clear an access road to the targeted area.

As soon as Alfonso and his family arrive at the hacienda, the reader discovers a world of unbelievable degradation and abuse. For Alfonso, Indians are expendable and exist only to satisfy his needs and interests. In fact, the Indians are mere chattel who occupy *huasipungos*, small plots of land on Alfonso's property. The *huasipungos* are the Indians' only source of sustenance, and in an arrangement reminiscent of feudal times, each occupant is obliged to obey and serve Alfonso, the prototypical landowner of the highlands.

With the completion of the road, the novel reaches its tragic climax. Alfonso and his business partners decide that they no longer need the Indians' labor. Instead, they now require a more technical and specialized workforce that must be accommodated on the *huasipungos*. The Indians rebel when told they must leave their land to make room for the outsiders. The uprising ends in a massacre as armed troops storm the occupied area.

Icaza wrote *Huasipungo* to shock and repulse his readers. On the one hand, the abuse meted out by Alfonso and his cohorts from the Catholic Church and the government is so absolute and extreme that readers could hardly ignore the need for fundamental changes in Ecuadorian society. At the same time, Icaza's descriptions of the Indians intentionally strip them of their humanity. They rarely speak, and for the most part they seem more like stray dogs than human beings.

While *Huasipungo* became a kind of call to arms and symbolized the Indian plight throughout Latin America, one could argue that creating solidarity and sympathy by dehumanizing the Indians actually reinforced negative stereotypes and racist attitudes among many readers. The outrage that Icaza provoked did not contribute to a greater appreciation of Indians as capable human beings or as viable partners worthy of respect in the continued development of the nation. Indians were victims, but they also came across as helpless, ignorant, and a source of collective shame.

Huasipungo and other *indigenista* novels played a major role in sensitizing readers to the corruption and abuse that characterized their governments and social institutions. As works of literature, however, many were basically flawed because few writers (and readers) really understood the inner lives of the Indians. Thus, the social message frequently eclipsed artistic expression and always undermined character development. It is no wonder that in 1928, the Peruvian writer José Carlos Mariátegui insisted on the differences between *indigenista* literature and a literature produced by Indians. Although he applauded efforts to champion Indian rights, he understood that readers would discover the richness and the complexities of the Indians only when the latter were able to speak for themselves.

Despite *Huasipungo*'s fame, *El chulla Romero y Flores* (1958)[2] is arguably Icaza's finest novel because it expresses the author's social and cultural milieu. No longer limited by the distance that separated him and other mestizo writers from their Indian subjects, Icaza succeeds in creating a group of characters who resonate far beyond the novel's social message. The psychological depth and complexity lacking in *Huasipungo* becomes, the driving force in *El chulla Romero y Flores*.

The novel explores the tensions and contradictions inherent in the cultural identity of Luis Alfonso Romero y Flores, a middle-class mestizo who struggles to reconcile his Indian and non-Indian heritages. The son of a humble Indian woman and a haughty father of Spanish ancestry, Luis Alfonso spends his life seeking social acceptance and advancement by publicly distancing himself from everything that might connect him to his mother. Obviously, Luis Alfonso's dilemma represents the conflict that has defined so much of Ecuador's broader search for national identity. In each case, climbing the proverbial social (or international) ladder has meant being less Indian and more European.

Through the use of interior monologue and fragmented time, Icaza leads his protagonist to self-discovery. The denial of his maternal heritage is part and parcel of a national inferiority complex that had its origins in the nineteenth-century debate over "civilization and barbarianism." Indeed, Icaza understood that such a false dichotomy had helped solidify a highly stratified society of haves and have-nots.

By the end of the novel, Luis Alfonso achieves a kind of psychological wholeness and overcomes his ambitions to enter the pretentious and arbitrary world of social privilege. By identifying himself with his class and racial peers, he accepts his own diversity as a source of growth and fulfillment. Symbolically, Icaza has drawn on his protagonist's experiences so that readers may comprehend the pluralistic nature of their own mestizo identity and, by extension, that of the nation.

AFRO-ECUADORIAN LITERATURE

Although many people identify Ecuador with its Indian roots, few understand the extent to which Blacks have been an integral part of the nation since the sixteenth century. Adalberto Ortiz (1914) and Nelson Estupiñán Bass (1912) are two writers who have done much to correct the oversight. Both have written literary works that are considered among the most important expressions of the African Diaspora published throughout the Americas.

Adalberto Ortiz (1914–   )

With the growing importance of social realism and *indigenismo* in Ecuadorian literature of the 1930s and 1940s, Adalberto Ortiz seized the opportunity to write about his native province of Esmeraldas, where the majority of Ecuadorian Blacks live. *Juyungo* (1943; *Juyungo*, 1982) is a classic bildungsroman about a young Black man who gradually discovers the complex web of racism as he searches for his place in mestizo Ecuador. Unlike so many *indigenista* novels, in which the Indian characters were little more than objects used to justify the author's protest, *Juyungo* was a tour de force of Afro-Ecuadorian culture and interracial/intraracial relations. Indeed, Ortiz drew upon his own experiences as a mulatto who has spent his entire life trying to balance his multiple identities (Black, mulatto, Ecuadorian).

Although Ortiz denounces many of the abuses and injustices that have filled other protest novels, his treatment of race has been controversial. During the 1930s and 1940s, social progressives sought to change Ecuadorian society by means of a united front (or social class) made up of workers and the poor. References to race and ethnicity could only break such unity, especially when arguing that a particular group has needs and interests that require unique solutions.

Ortiz did not intend *Juyungo* to be divisive. In fact, he has always insisted that his protagonist, Ascensión Lastre, is an Ecuadorian above all else. Ortiz's reaction clearly illustrates a fundamental problem inherent in all multicultural and multiracial societies. There is a fine line between national unity and a nation's diversity. Ascensión's search for identity throughout the novel symbolizes that delicate balance, particularly in light of the ambiguity and self-doubt that characterize him and several other characters.

Notwithstanding Ortiz's assurances that he had not broken with the social realists, *Juyungo* has proven to be both socially and artistically more complete than most *indigenista* and social protest novels because it openly addresses Ecuador's social and racial diversity. Furthermore, the novel's holistic depiction of Afro Ecuadorians and social change has enabled *Juyungo* to transcend its national boundaries and become a standard for using literature to interpret the African Diaspora.

Nelson Estupiñán Bass (1912–   )

While Ortiz has been cautious about expressing his blackness in ways that might antagonize readers who view any racial discourse as divisive and even racist, Nelson Estupiñán Bass has assumed a more aggressive position in defense of his racial identity. That is not to say that he is any less Ecuadorian or less concerned about society misconstruing his views on race and nationality than Ortiz. Estupiñán Bass has not defined himself as a mulatto, and therefore his artistic and social discourse has never been ambiguous about who he is or why social change must take race and ethnicity into account.

Like Ortiz, Estupiñán Bass has written both fiction and poetry, and he, too, has established himself as a major literary figure within the African Diaspora. One of his most representative works is his first novel, *Cuando los guayacanes florecían* (1954; *When the Guayacanes Were in Bloom*, 1987). Based on a historical uprising led by a Black, Colonel Carlos Concha, at the beginning of the twentieth century, the novel focuses on Blacks from Esmeraldas who continue to be victimized by servitude. In addition to experiencing the abuses suffered by all oppressed people, Estupiñán Bass's characters understand that their race is inextricably connected to their social condition.

Unlike characters in many of the social protest and *indigenista* novels in particular, Estupiñán's characters do not look for solutions outside of their own community and traditions. They are portrayed as agents of change rather than defenseless children in need of surrogate masters. Moreover, Estupiñán Bass successfully avoids simplistic dichotomies; corruption and deceit are not extraneous to Blacks and their behavior, nor are heroism and the ability to solve problems characteristic only of non-Blacks.

A careful and comprehensive reading of the works by Ortiz and Estupiñán Bass (and by other Afro-Ecuadorian writers like the poet Antonio Preciado) reveals that the Afro presence in Ecuador is not peripheral to the national experience. Moreover, their work is a reminder that prejudice and fallacious stereotypes must be confronted by all segments of society. Clearly, national unity should not be the product of denying diversity; rather, it must grow out of a multicultural and multiracial society capable of forging a common project of justice and mutual respect.

ECUADOR'S CULTURAL RENAISSANCE

By the 1950s, Ecuador's Golden Age of literature had run its course. The principal themes and innovative techniques that characterized the best of social realism and much of the protest literature written in the 1930s and 1940s had become stale and formulaic. Despite such exceptions as Icaza's *El chulla Romero y Flores* and Estupiñán Bass's *Cuando los guayacanes florecían*, Ecuadorian literature lacked the iconoclastic spirit of the previous generation. Furthermore, there was no common project to unite writers and channel their creative energies. Instead, the economic prosperity from banana exports of the 1950s and the apparent political stability of the decade plunged literature into a state of conformity where few writers dared to look beyond the canonized models.

With the advent of the 1960s, however, a new generation of writers appeared in Ecuador. They referred to their overarching project as cultural parricide, and with an irreverence that was characteristic of the times, these young writers questioned the value and merit of the country's cultural institutions and literary traditions. Among their first objectives was destruction of the notions that writers were superior to other workers and that literature was more noble or valuable than other forms of work. Spontaneous poetry readings sprang up in public plazas, and many writers joined grassroots organizations as they searched for effective ways to democratize cultural production in general.

One of the first groups to take the lead in redefining the role of the intellectual in a developing country such as Ecuador was the *Tzántzicos* (head-shrinkers). This group from Quito insisted that writers dedicate their art to carrying out fundamental structural changes in Ecuadorian society. In many ways, the *Tzántzicos* had taken up the social action agenda that the Grupo de Guayaquil and other social realists of the 1930s had championed. The younger writers recognized, however, that many good intentions of the past had never been put into practice. Moreover, too many iconoclasts and self-proclaimed revolutionaries had allowed themselves to be co-opted by powerful public and private institutions. The *Tzántzicos* were committed to reaffirming the writer's subversive and antiestablishment role precisely because the majority of Ecuador's citizens remained on the social and economic fringes of society.

After an initial period of protest, militancy, and innumerable actions designed to shock a public that had become too passive and too indifferent to the nation's social and financial problems, the *Tzántzicos* joined forces with other young progressives in 1968 to form the Frente Cultural (Cultural Front). Whereas earlier activities were often spontaneous happenings, the Frente Cultural turned its attention to elaborating a more disciplined and studied approach to writing a literature that would be both socially and artistically revolutionary. To that end, between 1972 and 1977, the Frente Cultural published *Bufanda del Sol* (The Sun's Scarf), a literary review in which writers cultivated an ongoing analysis of their craft.

Bufanda del Sol contributed enormously to the explosive resurgence of Ecuadorian literature in the 1970s. In fact, many of the review's principal contributors would become leading novelists and poets in both Ecuador and Latin America during the last quarter of the twentieth century. Iván Egüez, Raúl Pérez, Abdón Ubidia, Iván Carvajal, and Fernando Tinajero are just a few of the writers who illustrate the extent to which *Bufanda del Sol* served as a kind of laboratory for the creation of an innovative and invigorated literature.

Ecuador's cultural renaissance of the 1970s was due in large part to the sudden economic growth created by the oil boom. Plentiful resources meant that an increasing number of public and private institutions were eager to support the arts. It would be an egregious error, however, to suggest that Ecuador's literary boom was merely the result of an economic bonanza. The writers whose works began to appear in the 1970s had in fact served a long apprenticeship during which they assimilated many of the innovations that had characterized the best literature written in Ecuador and the rest of Latin America since the 1930s. Jorge Luis Borges, Julio Cortázar, Alejo Carpentier, José Donoso, Mario Vargas Llosa, Gabriel García Márquez, Carlos Fuentes, Octavio Paz, Pablo Neruda, and the Grupo de Guayaquil constituted an invaluable resource without which contemporary writers could not have rejuvenated Ecuadorian literature.

Pablo Palacio and the New Ecuadorian Narrative

Ecuador's Pablo Palacio (1906–1947) was among the writers of the previous generation who most affected the coming of age of Ecuador's contemporary narrative fiction. Because he wrote during the height of social realism, when writers believed that an authentic national literature had to deal with the country's masses, readers greatly misunderstood and underestimated the importance of Palacio's work. His fiction was about Ecuador's emerging middle class, an urban petite bourgeoisie that had lost its way in a trivial existence devoid of human compassion and solidarity. In an era characterized by broad social causes, Palacio seemed obtuse and disengaged. His narrative world of alienation and cynicism so patently evident in *Débora* (1929) and *Vida del ahorcado* (1932; The Life of the Hanged Man) struck readers as decadent and socially irresponsible.

By the 1960s, however, readers began to appreciate Palacio's mastery of irony, parody, and ambiguity more fully. They finally discovered in Palacio a self-reflexivity that converted his work into a form of metafiction in which the creative process had become the principal subject of each text. That is to say, Palacio was writing about writing. More important, he was experimenting with fiction to establish the middle-class writer and his urban context as being just as essential in the creation of a national literature as the Indians, the Blacks, and the dispossessed in general.

Despite good intentions, many of the literary works that championed social causes on behalf of the masses were artificial and shallow because the writers allowed the message to overshadow their forms of expression. Palacio, however, never attempted to reproduce reality directly. He understood that fiction was primarily a creation of language, and as such, its effectiveness would depend on the writer's ability to suggest meaning through connotations. One might best describe Palacio's legacy by paraphrasing an observation that García Márquez made about his own writing: writers distort reality so that readers may see it more clearly.

ECUADORIAN CONTEMPORARY FICTION: AN OVERVIEW

Since the 1970s, Ecuador has produced many outstanding literary works that have masterfully combined their social message with compelling literary forms. This literature has demanded that readers actively engage the text by completing each author's oblique references with their own creative interpretations. In fact, one could argue that the principal difference between today's literature and the literature written before the 1970s has to do with the changed relationship between writers and readers. Be that as it may, it is abundantly clear that the best of Ecuadorian literature has evolved from many sources, past and present. Moreover, one must be careful not to categorize an evolving literature in rigid dualistic terms (i.e., the old versus the new). Indeed, some of the most innovative features of Ecuador's contemporary literature had already appeared in the fiction of Cuadra, Aguilera Malta, and Palacio.

There are certainly many writers of the contemporary period who deserve mention, and no list can really do justice to the breadth and quality of Ecuador's literature since 1975. What follows is a brief description of four writers who in many ways are representative of the larger corpus of literary production in contemporary Ecuador. Each has won national and international literary prizes; all four are among Ecuador's most productive writers; and their themes and writing techniques confirm the extent to which Ecuadorian literature is an integral part of Latin American letters.

Jorge Enrique Adoum (1923–   )

Jorge Enrique Adoum and his novel *Entre Marx y una mujer desnuda* (1976; Between Marx and a Naked Woman) illustrate the extent to which Ecuadorian literature constitutes a continuum of themes and influences. Adoum is one of the most renowned and multifaceted writers Ecuador has produced during the last half of the twentieth century. In his youth, he was Pablo Neruda's personal secretary; later, he worked for some twenty years for UNESCO in Paris, and during that time, he established close friendships with such Latin American luminaries as Julio Cortázar, Alejo Carpentier, and Gabriel García Márquez.

Besides his international reputation as a writer, Adoum personally knew Ecuador's original social realists; he thus occupies a unique position in Ecuadorian contemporary letters. *Entre Marx y una mujer desnuda* reflects Adoum's broad experience: it is a novel based on the life of the Grupo de Guayaquil's Gallegos Lara, and it employs many of the narrative techniques commonly found in Latin America's most celebrated novels published since the 1960s. Basically, it is a novel about writing a novel; that is, it is about a novelist who is struggling to write. Through the course of the novel, Adoum blurs the traditional boundaries between author/protagonist and author/reader. To carry out his project, he fragments time, utilizes parallel stories from diverse points of view, incorporates pictures and reprints from newspapers into his text, inserts notes to comment on the creative process, and even offers, simultaneously, two renditions of a single incident. In effect, his innovative approach to evoking a part of Ecuador's literary heritage is a vivid reminder of just how connected the present is with the past. In 1977, *Entre Marx y una mujer desnuda* won Mexico's Xavier Villaurrutia Prize for Latin American fiction.

Alicia Yánez Cossío (1929–)

In 1973, Alicia Yánez Cossío published her groundbreaking novel *Bruna, soroche y los tíos* (Bruna, Altitude Sickness, and Relatives), which had won a national prize as an outstanding novel in 1972. The novel is about a young woman who rebels against a patriarchal society and becomes a kind of clarion for social change. Bruna is not only a symbol of the emergence of a new woman in search of a more meaningful lifestyle, she also constitutes a role model for all youth who must accept the challenge of creating a new society capable of succeeding in the modern world.

Since the publication of *Bruna, soroche y los tíos*, Yánez Cossío has written eight more novels in which she has used a variety of narrative styles and techniques. In her novels parody and irony frequently create a burlesque humor that brings into question many of society's traditional mores and values. In general, the power of her novels lies in her ability to capture the complexities and contradictions that characterize the struggle to achieve a balance between the best of the old and the new. While she makes clear that continuing to live in the past threatens to asphyxiate her characters through its taboos and anachronistic conventions, she also warns against blindly sacrificing traditional values for the gold and glitter of consumerism.

There is no question that Yánez Cossío is one of Ecuador's leading contemporary novelists. Because many of her works have been translated into other languages, her readership is no longer limited to Ecuador or to the Spanish-speaking world. In 1996, she received France's Sor Juana Inés de la Cruz Prize for her novel *El Cristo feo* (1995; The Ugly Christ).

Eliécer Cárdenas (1950)

Eliécer Cárdenas is one of Ecuador's most prolific contemporary writers. His most famous novel, *Polvo y ceniza* (1978; Dust and Ashes) is arguably the finest novel written in Ecuador since 1950. It focuses on the popular legend of Naún Briones, a Robin Hoodesque bandit from Ecuador's southern highlands. As Cárdenas reconstructs his story from a mixture of historical accounts and popular beliefs, he brings into question the whole issue of morality and ethical behavior. Unlike the urban criminal and petty thief El Aguila (the Eagle), Naún steals to help the downtrodden and the impoverished. In effect, Cárdenas uses his fiction to subvert the prevailing social order by converting an apparent social misfit into an epic hero.

Perhaps even more interesting is the way in which Cárdenas re-creates the internal conflict of the epic hero. While the poor look to Naún as their savior and believe in his invincibility, he finds himself struggling with his image, an image created by others. Even in his own mind, the distinction between fiction and reality becomes blurred. Paradoxically, it is his fame of mythic proportions that gradually isolates him from the very people who revere him. *Polvo y ceniza* reveals a complex web of contradictions; solitude and solidarity are the forces that bring together and ultimately separate the common people from their heroes.

Jorge Velasco Mackenzie (1949–)

The two principal concerns that form the basis of Jorge Velasco Mackenzie's fiction are his fascination with the sociocultural milieu of Guayaquil's poor and the close relationship that exists between history and fiction. *El Rincón de los Justos* (1983; The Corner of the Just) depicts the life of a group of tenement dwellers in Guayaquil. Together, the characters evoke a vital part of the growing city's past and present. References to well-known movie houses, plazas, flea markets, and bars re-create an atmosphere that is unmistakably Guayaquil. More important, Velasco Mackenzie allows his characters to narrate their story in their own language. Street slang and sexually charged expressions reinforce the vitality and creativity of the novel's subjects. Furthermore, Velasco Mackenzie's effective use of language subverts many of society's traditional prejudices concerning proper usage. Although there is much suffering in *El Rincón de los Justos*, Velasco is never patronizing; respect and compassion are the driving forces behind his portrait of Guayaquil's dispossessed.

Velasco Mackenzie turned his attention to history when writing *Tambores para una canción perdida* (1986; Drums for a Lost Song). Basically, the novel deals with a runaway slave and the Afro presence in Ecuadorian history. By mixing African myths with historical events, Velasco Mackenzie uses his fiction to revise a portion of the country's official history that, generally speaking, has been loath to accept its African roots.

Tambores para una canción perdida was the first of several projected historical novels. In 1996, Velasco Mackenzie published *En nombre de un amor imaginario* (In The Name of an Imaginary Love), a novel about the international team of scientists that came to Ecuador to chart the equator during the eighteenth century. Again, Velasco Mackenzie offers an alternative view to Ecuador's official history. Through fiction, he debunks the myth of the noble and disinterested scientist, and shows that passion, greed, and fame are as much a part of science as is the search for truth and knowledge.

CONCLUSION

Despite the many obstacles that have made writing and publishing difficult in Ecuador, this chapter clearly shows that *"¡Ecuador sí escribe!"* ("Ecuador does, in fact, write!"). With rare exceptions, the best of Ecuadorian literature has been socially engaged. Socially committed literature, however, does not negate the aesthetic dimension of artistic creation. Ecuador's most memorable works are those in which society and literature complement one another.

NOTES

1. Ecuadorians are not very precise in their usage of the terms *cholo* and *montuvio*. Basically, both refer to people of Indian and white blood. Coastal people living in river areas are generally referred to as *montuvios* instead of *cholos*.

2. *Chulla* refers to a middle-class man or woman who tries to climb the social ladder by imitating the upper class's mores.

REFERENCES

Barrera, Isaac. *Historia de la literatura Ecuatoriana*. Quito: Libresa, 1979.

Cueva, Agustín. *Entre la ira y la esperanza: Ensayos sobre la cultura nacional*. Cuenca: Editorial Casa de la Cultura Ecuatoriana, 1981.

———. *Lecturas y rupturas*. Quito: Editorial Planeta, 1986.

Donoso Pareja, Miguel. *Los grandes de la década del '30*. Quito: Editorial El Conejo, 1985.

Handelsman, Michael. *Incursiones en el mundo literario del Ecuador*. Guayaquil: Universidad de Guayaquil, 1987.

———. *Lo afro y la plurinacionalidad: El caso ecuatoriano visto desde su literatura*. Oxford, MS: Romance Monographs, 1999.

Harrison, Regina. *Entre el tronar épico y el llanto elegíaco: Simbología indígena en la poesía Ecuatoriana de los siglos XIX–XX*. Quito: Ediciones Abya-Yala y Universidad Andina Simón Bolívar, 1996.

Rodríguez Castelo, Hernán, Cecilia Ansaldo, Diego Araujo, and Alejandro Moreano. *La literatura Ecuatoriana en los últimos 30 años (1950–1980)*. Quito: Editorial El Conejo, 1983.

Tinajero, Fernando. *Aproximaciones y distancias*. Quito: Editorial Planeta, 1986.

Waag, Michael. "The Ecuadorian Novel of the 1970s in the Context of Its Historical and Literary Past." Ph.D. diss., University of Illinois, 1983.

7

Performing Arts

The performing arts in Ecuador have experienced many of the same problems as cinema and literature. Insufficient resources and an ineffective infrastructure in both the public and private sectors have greatly hampered production and promotion. To the extent that professionalization is a criterion used to evaluate the quality and importance of the performing arts in Ecuador, the picture is very pessimistic. On the one hand, the more intellectual productions rarely provide enough opportunities for practitioners to earn an adequate living. On the other hand, struggling popular and commercial artists are too often stereotyped as bohemians who shun "real employment" (Campos 432). In either case, career artists are few in number and, generally speaking, their dedication and talent are undervalued by the majority of Ecuadorians.

In face of the bleak social and economic conditions that all artists confront in Ecuador, one cannot help but admire those who have refused to be silenced or deterred. Their resolve and creativity have ensured that music, dance, and theater continue to be an integral part of Ecuadorian life. Moreover, each performance—whether in an exclusive theater or in a public square—constitutes a testimony that cultural expression is fundamental to the human experience. Regardless of the many hardships endured by the people, or the zealous cries for practical (i.e., profitable) objectives in education and government, the performing arts continue to fill a void in consumer-driven Ecuador.

MUSIC

Although there are no absolute boundaries between the various performing arts, music has evolved and developed more fully than dance or theater in Ecuador. Music does not depend as much on staging or on group participation. Consequently, in terms of both listening and performing, music has proven to be more accessible to the public.

Music's origins in Ecuador can be traced to pre-Columbian times. Archaeologists have found whistles in numerous excavation sites along the Coast, and musicologists have identified musical traditions in the Andean highlands that predate the Spanish conquest and colonization (Guevara 46). The early indigenous music was deeply anchored in community life. Appropriate forms accompanied religious celebrations, planting, harvesting, and warfare. Along with numerous kinds of flutes, the most characteristic instruments of the period, small pieces of metal struck together and human shouts gave music its rhythmic qualities (Guevara 47).

One of the world's most primitive forms of music has been attributed to the Shuar Indians of the Amazon region. These people produced only three or four sounds. According to the occasion or the circumstances, however, the Shuar demonstrated an ability to create a rich variety of rhythms and a diverse range of melodic tones (Guevara 47).

To the Spanish conquerors and colonizers, indigenous music sounded infernal, pagan, warlike, and mournful. Consequently, church authorities frequently prohibited native music. Moreover, because the church was wary of cultural traditions and practices that could threaten its evangelical conquest of Indian souls, officials sometimes destroyed instruments that had been used in native rituals (Guerrero Gutiérrez, *Músicos del Ecuador* v).

The music that would dominate in these clashes of cultures was the religious music of the fourteenth and fifteenth centuries that the Spanish missionaries brought to America. This music was primarily played in the European convents and monasteries, where a leading priest served as the choir master or principal composer, interpreter, and music teacher. That tradition was followed in America. In fact, at the beginning of the colonial period, only ordained priests from Spain were acceptable choices for choir master (Guerrero Gutiérrez, *Músicos del Ecuador* vi).

By the end of the sixteenth century, professional musicians began to replace the priests as music directors and teachers. Because many of these musicians were creoles and even mestizos, they were likely to enrich the musical repertoire with indigenous traditions, albeit subtly. In time, music

developed into something far more than a means of evangelization and ac-
culturation.

Just as had occurred in the rest of America, in Ecuador diverse musical
idioms converged to create unique and innovative forms. Notwithstanding
the official policies of colonization that the Spanish Crown and the Catholic
Church had established, America eclipsed royal and ecclesiastical absolutisms,
especially with regard to cultural expression. In fact, in Ecuador, music's
pluralism emerged in 1535, when two Franciscan monks began teaching
music to Indians. Although the latter assimilated the European and Catholic
musical traditions, the constant interaction between peoples led to musical
fusion.

Religious music was not the only form to reach Ecuador, nor were the
clergy the only ones to bring music with them from Spain. To be sure, Spain
was the principal musical influence in Ecuador until the end of the eighteenth
century, when the waltz, the minuet, and the cotillion became popular. However, Spanish secular and popular music, which was highly diverse and multifaceted, was extremely influential outside of the church's domain as early as
the sixteenth century. The guitar, for example, played a vital role in producing musical syncetism in Ecuador. From the moment indigenous rhythms
like the *sanjuanitos, yaravíes,* and *albazos* were adapted to the guitar, a foundation for Ecuadorian music began to emerge (Guerrero Gutiérrez, *Músicos
del Ecuador* x).

Although musical interactions occurred frequently and widely during the
colonial period, there is no concrete evidence that Ecuadorians produced
their own musical compositions during the centuries preceding independence. It has been argued, however, that the absence of historical documentation and authored compositions does not indicate a lack of musical creativity.
Rather, these voids are the result of musical and cultural institutions that
have shown little interest in the research and preservation of Ecuador's musical heritage (Guerrero Gutiérrez *Músicos del Ecuador* x–xi).

Be that as it may, music in Ecuador formally and systematically assumed
its own national character during the nineteenth century. Both the establish-
ment of the National Conservatory of Music in Quito in 1870 and the
formation of military bands contributed enormously to establishing music as
a genuine expression of Ecuador's national identity (Guerrero Gutiérrez, *Músicos del Ecuador* xi). Just as literature and painting had been transformed by
nineteenth-century nationalism, so music emerged from church cloisters and
oral folk traditions.

Indeed, a new nation required specific cultural markers that would distinguish it from the rest of the world. The issue of identity was especially significant for Ecuador, a country whose territorial boundaries were not officially resolved until 1999. Moreover, even after independence in 1822, Ecuador was initially the Southern District within Gran Colombia until 1830. Consequently, for Ecuador, nation-building implied much more than political sovereignty.

With respect to music, the urgency of national definition inspired many Ecuadorian musicians to pay closer attention to their indigenous musical roots as they searched for ways to leave a uniquely Ecuadorian imprint on music. At the same time, a growing number of Ecuadorians understood that having a cadre of musicians who could master European classical music would be an affirmation of national distinction and pride.

Classical Music and the Ecuadorian Context

Initially, the Ecuadorian government hired foreigners as music instructors and band directors. They were charged with establishing a musical infrastructure that would legitimize Ecuador as a bona fide member of the family of "civilized" nations. Musicians struggled with the same dilemmas and contradictions that characterized their literary counterparts: during an intensely nationalist era, many intellectuals felt compelled to measure their worth in terms of European values and traditions.

Like the other arts, music evolved as Ecuadorians searched for ways to balance their European and native heritages. One of the first to succeed in this process was Segundo Luis Moreno (1882–1974). He studied clarinet, musical theory, and composition at the National Conservatory from 1906 to 1913. By 1915, he was director of several military bands, a position that allowed him to travel throughout Ecuador and to discover the country's diverse musical traditions. More important, because band directors were full-time military officials, Moreno was gainfully employed and could devote himself entirely to music.

Throughout his career as a musician and musicologist, Moreno insisted on highlighting the beauty and richness of Ecuadorian music. As he became an expert in Ecuadorian folklore and music, he arranged and composed a musical repertoire for his bands that combined the indigenous and the classical. In addition to many marches, he produced orchestral pieces such as his *Suite Ecuatoriana*, which adapted Indian prayer music to classical forms and techniques. One of his principal contributions to Ecuadorian music was his three-volume *Historia de la música en el Ecuador*. (The first volume was published in 1972; the remaining volumes are still unpublished.)

Francisco Salgado Ayala (1880–1970) was one of Moreno's most distinguished colleagues and classmates at the National Conservatory of Music. A composer and pianist, Salgado was heavily influenced by the nineteenth-century Polish composer Frédéric Chopin at the beginning of his career. In fact, Ayala's first compositions for piano included waltzes and polonaises that clearly evoked their European source. Like Moreno, however, Salgado turned his attention to Ecuador's indigenous roots. His many musical compositions, textbooks, and monographs constitute a vital resource for Ecuadorian ethnomusicology. Furthermore, Salgado's work as a musician and musicologist clearly demonstrates the degree to which classical and native musical forms transcend artificial dichotomies. In time, other Ecuadorians (and the rest of the world) would discover the beauty of indigenous flutes playing Bach or European orchestras interpreting native rhythms and melodies.

Luis Humberto Salgado (1903–1977) was the third outstanding composer who emerged from the National Conservatory of Music at the beginning of the twentieth century. With Segundo Luis Moreno, and with his father, Francisco Salgado Ayala, he helped lay the foundation for classical music in Ecuador. The younger Salgado wrote eight symphonies, four operas, three ballets, and numerous pieces for chamber orchestras. He, too, developed a deep appreciation for Ecuador's indigenous heritage. In fact, one of his operas was based on the *indianista* novel *Cumandá*, which Juan León Mera had written at the height of Ecuadorian romanticism in 1879.

While directing military bands offered his father and Moreno financial stability and the opportunity to devote themselves exclusively to music, Luis Humberto Salgado originally found his niche playing piano to accompany silent movies. Later, he became the director of numerous musical institutes and orchestras, including the National Conservatory in 1952. Salgado also distinguished himself as a music critic; he wrote for Quito's principal newspaper, *El Comercio*, and for Spain's music journal *Ritmo*.

The musical influence of Moreno and the two Salgados was undoubtedly decisive in the development of classical music in Ecuador. As musicians, teachers, and ethnomusicologists, their work stands as a legacy that has inspired many Ecuadorians to commit a part of their lives to classical music, either as performers or as knowledgeable listeners. Furthermore, their combined efforts to work with European and native musical traditions have, in no small measure, demonstrated the relevance and beauty of all forms of music.

Despite the financial, political, and social crises inherent in their country, Ecuadorians have found ways to honor the legacy left by Moreno and the Salgados. Ecuador officially established a National Symphonic Orchestra in

1950. Financial and political considerations, however, prevented the inaugural concert from taking place until 1956. The Symphony's first director was Ernesto Xancó, a cellist from Spain. By 1990, numerous organizations had been founded to sponsor musical training and research. Especially noteworthy were Quito's Metropolitan Symphonic Band and the Orchestra for Andean Musical Instruments. As of 1995, the government was sponsoring approximately 20 music institutes throughout the country (Guerrero Gutiérrez, *Músicos del Ecuador* xvii–xviii).

Milton Estévez (1947–   ), Arturo Rodas (1951–   ), Diego Luzuriaga (1955–   ), and Alvaro Manzano (1955–   ) are among Ecuador's composers who have established themselves as leading figures during the last quarter of the twentieth century. Estévez, Rodas, and Luzuriaga have followed similar paths. They began their training at the National Conservatory in Quito, and later they studied electrical acoustic music and composition in France. Estévez, a classical guitarist, earned first prize for music composition at the Ecole Normale de Musique de Paris in 1984. Rodas has devoted much of his efforts to introducing Ecuadorians to contemporary musical forms and techniques through seminars and journal articles. Luzuriaga, in addition to many musical compositions for strings, flute, and piano, has written important essays on Ecuadorian folk music.

Alvaro Manzano, originally from Ambato, has been the conductor of the National Symphonic Orchestra since 1985. He traveled to the Soviet Union in 1975 to study choral conducting. In 1979, he entered the Tchaikovsky Conservatory of Music in Moscow, where he completed his studies in 1985, graduating with the title of Conductor of Symphonic Orchestras and Opera. In 1991, Manzano was honored in Helsinki, Finland, as one of the world's outstanding young musicians. He has been visiting conductor of symphonic orchestras in Bolivia, Peru, Colombia, Argentina, the Dominican Republic, and Iceland.

Popular Music

Like Ecuador's classical musicians, who have rarely distanced themselves from their native musical roots, popular musicians have created a national music primarily from Indian and Spanish sources. The *sanjuanito*, the *pasacalle*, and the *pasillo* are three of the best-known rhythms and melodies that make up Ecuadorian music. The hybrid nature of the music is especially dynamic because the musical fusion rarely obscures the richness and integrity of each component. From a social and cultural perspective, it might be argued that Ecuadorian popular music symbolizes the potential for pluralist societies to cultivate their diversity in an atmosphere of interaction and fluidity. Indeed, the power of Ecuadorian music lies in its ability to express Ecuador's many identities harmoniously.

The *sanjuanito* is festive and especially popular at dances. Although there is much speculation about its origins, it appears that the music can be traced to the religious celebrations of both Catholics and Indians on or about June 24, the feast day of Saint John the Baptist. *Sanjuanito* (Little Saint John) is an obvious reference to the Catholic Church's religious calendar; however, Saint John's Day coincided with the Indian celebration of *Inti raymi*. Thus, while the music carries a Hispanic name, the primary musical source was Indian (Guerrero Gutiérrez 1997, 63–64). The *sanjuanito* is an example of how the church appropriated Indian religious practices by incorporating them into its own traditions.

The *pasacalle* is an adaptation of the Spanish *pasodoble*. It began evolving in the nineteenth century and flourished at the beginning of the twentieth century. The music is basically written in 2/4 time and is danced with lots of movement. The social and festive nature of the *pasacalle* can probably be attributed, in part, to the fact that Spanish *pasodobles* were played at bullfights, which were community happenings full of energy and vitality. (During the colonial period, Ecuadorians had adopted bullfighting as an integral part of many of their principal civic and religious celebrations.) In general, one dances the *pasacalle* by stepping forward and backward, and then turning to the left and to the right; arms are raised and slightly bent as the male holds his partner's hands at shoulder height (Guerrero Gutiérrez 1997, 62).

Unlike the *sanjuanito* and *pasacalle*, the *pasillo* has a slow tempo and is usually played in a minor key. It dates to the middle of the nineteenth century, when it was also popular in Venezuela and Colombia. The *pasillo*, which means "short step," is supposedly an adaptation of the waltz. More important, however, in Ecuador (as well as in other parts of Latin America) the *pasillo* evolved into one of the most popular musical forms that was used for love songs (Guerrero Gutiérrez, "Tonos y bailes del Ecuador" 62).

In Ecuador, those who have composed and/or sung *pasillos* are legion. Moreover, the *pasillo* has contributed enormously to the development of Ecuador's prosperous music industry. One of the first success stories occurred in 1930, when Guayaquil's Dúo Ecuador traveled to New York to record for Columbia House. Nicasio Safadi and Enrique Ibáñez Mora composed and performed their own music. Among the songs they recorded for Columbia House was the highly popular "Guayaquil de mis amores" (Guayaquil of My Loves).

Although the first known recordings registered in Ecuador date to 1912, the recording industry did not really take off until 1946, when the Fadisa Record Company began mass-producing its recordings. Fadisa's first record was "En las lejanías" (In Faraway Places), a *pasillo* that Rubira Infante wrote and later intepreted with Olimpo Cárdenas (Guerrero Gutiérrez, *Músicos del Ecuador* xvi). These two musicians may be best remembered for the help they gave a young aspiring singer from Guayaquil, Julio Jaramillo.

Julio Jaramillo (1935–1978) was referred to as J. J. (pronounced in Spanish as *jota jota*). Few Ecuadorians have achieved as much international recognition and fame as Jaramillo. His popularity reached mythic proportions, and when he died at the age of 43 tens of thousands of Ecuadorians attended his funeral in Guayaquil. Since his death, numerous short stories, poems, and parts of novels have been based on his life.

J. J. recorded more than 4,000 songs, many of which were *pasillos*. In fact, his birth date (October 1) has been officially declared the Day of the Ecuadorian *Pasillo* (Guerrero Gutiérrez, *Músicos del Ecuador* 90). Most of his songs were about failed promises and unrequited love. His bohemian lifestyle captured the imagination of a *machista* (excessively virile) society that rejoiced in celebrating the trials and tribulations of a womanizer, heavy smoker, and excessive drinker. Moreover, his falsetto voice seemed to express everyone's weaknesses and mortality. For Ecuadorians, Julio Jaramillo and the *pasillo* continue to be as glorious as Argentina's Carlos Gardel and the tango, or as mesmerizing as the United States' Frank Sinatra and the ballad.

After the turbulent 1960s, many young musicians throughout Latin America turned their attention to socially committed forms of musical expression. The New Song movement took Latin Americans back to their folk roots; the goal was to connect with the common people while creating a more just and democratic society. Indeed, protest and social realism were not new experiences for Ecuadorians. Literature and painting had already become paragons for combining the aesthetic and the ethical. And most of Ecuador's musicians had never wandered very far from the common folk.

One of Ecuador's most successful musical groups within the New Song movement has been Pueblo Nuevo (New People). Originally from the southern region of Loja, the group adopted its name in 1975. On the cover of its compact disc *Cajita de música* (Little Music Box), Pueblo Nuevo explained that "art is a reflection of society, and by raising people's consciousness, art can help bring about change in that society." A renewed interest in Andean instruments, a rejuvenated appreciation of folk music from indigenous and Spanish sources, and an unwavering revolutionary spirit have been the basic ingredients for Pueblo Nuevo's musical accomplishments and success.

Music in Ecuador continues to have a dynamic and far-reaching presence.

More than 120 musical instruments and some 150 melodies and rhythms form the basis of Ecuador's diverse musical repertoire (Guerrero Gutiérrez, *Músicos del Ecuador* 197–202). In addition to its Indian, Spanish, and African heritages, Ecuadorian music has always been open to outside influences. Moreover, Ecuador's musicians and performers have been able to appropriate those influences while creating their own distinct (pluri)national idiom. Indeed, Chopin and Julio Jaramillo, fugues and *pasillos*, and French horns and marimbas have come together harmoniously at the center of the world.

THEATER

Unlike the other arts, that flourished under the tutelage of the church during the colonial period, theater never established itself as a viable art form or genre. Although theater did fit into the church's missionary project of religious conversion, performances rarely amounted to much more than didactic and moralistic monologues or dialogues that accompanied religious celebrations. The lackluster history of theater in Ecuador is an enigma. In the first place, some 160 dramatists and 700 titles have been registered in Ricardo Descalzi's *Critical History of Ecuadorian Theater*. At the same time, it is clear that Spanish plays were performed regularly in colonial Ecuador, especially in Quito (Descalzi 349). Nevertheless, despite the apparent activity and presence of theater in colonial times, there is no evidence of an emerging Ecuadorian theater (Descalzi 350).

Little has changed through the centuries. Time and time again theater initiates have lamented the lack of adequate locales, theater companies, and financial resources to stage productions. Closer examination reveals that a basic shortcoming of Ecuadorian theater has been its inconsistency. Unlike the other arts, that offer a legacy of interrelated traditions from which artists have evolved through the centuries, theater has had a history characterized by disjuncture. Indeed, successful efforts to produce theater have rarely been the outgrowth of previous achievements.

The inability to sustain promising initiatives, on the one hand, and the failure to lay a foundation of artistic roots, on the other, should not suggest an absence of talent, creativity, or even public interest in the theater. Despite the many obstacles, there have been some significant high points in the history of Ecuadorian theater. The construction in 1887 of Quito's beautiful and elaborate Teatro Sucre, for example, was a catalyst for all of the performing arts. With regard to theater specifically, the building's elegance has attracted important companies from abroad to perform in Ecuador. One can also argue that even during periods of inactivity, the Teatro Sucre's prominent location has served to keep alive the importance of theater in the minds of Ecuadorians.

Theater in Ecuador did flourish during the 1920s and 1930s. As numerous distinguished Spanish and Mexican companies staged plays, talented novelists and poets were inspired to write for the theater (Descalzi 354). Jorge Icaza, one of Ecuador's most widely read novelists, began his literary career as an actor. By 1928, he was writing dramatic plays. Demetrio Aguilera Malta, another one of Ecuador's literary luminaries, also experimented with theater in the 1930s. In fact, he eventually wrote such memorable plays as *El tigre* (The Tiger), *Dientes blancos* (White Teeth), and *Infierno negro* (Black Hell).

Beginning in 1935, Ecuador saw the emergence of a highly popular form of theater called the *estampa quiteña* (Quito sketch). Basically, these sketches were lighthearted representations of Quito's lower middle class. Full of satire and self-deprecating humor, the *estampas* were rooted in many of Quito's social customs and mannerisms. Clearly, their popularity, which spanned several decades, was largely due to Ernesto Albán, one of Ecuador's most renowned actors, who used the *estampas quiteñas* to create his stage persona— *el chulla quiteño*. Difficult to translate into English, *chulla* refers to an individual who uses his wits to move up the social ladder (Descalzi 356). Albán's satirical humor and portrayal of the *chulla*, who ridicules society's pretensions, hypocrisies, and peccadillos, might be best described as a cross between Will Rogers, Red Skelton, and Red Foxx.

During the 1950s and 1960s, Francisco Tobar García from Quito and José Martínez Queirolo from Guayaquil established themselves as leading dramatists in Ecuador. In addition to writing dozens of plays, they formed and developed repertory groups, staged and financed productions, and became outspoken advocates of public and private support for theater.

With the impetus gained from the Cuban Revolution (1959) and the iconoclastic 1960s, there arose considerable interest in experimental theater. Groups appeared throughout the country, especially in Quito and Guayaquil. For many, the goal was to eliminate the artificial barriers between actors and spectators. Theater was viewed as a means to move people to action. At times, actors interacted with the audience; on other occasions, plays were performed in public plazas.

Paradoxically, it was the military government that came to power in 1963 which allowed theater to move in new directions. Despite its repressive measures against leftist intellectuals and institutions, the government hired Fabio Paccioni, an Italian expert on theater and performance, to teach in Ecuador. Under his guidance, Ecuadorian theater entered an ideological phase in which practitioners questioned the ways that theater had been conceptualized and performed (Ribadeneira 121).

Paccioni worked out of the Casa de la Cultura Ecuatoriana in Quito, where he formed two theater groups: the Teatro Ensayo (Experimental Theater) and the Teatro Popular (People's Theater). While the first group experimented with the technical aspects of performance, the second group devoted itself to creating a theater that would be anchored in the daily lives of Ecuador's common folk. This latter project had very little to do with representing quaint cultural customs and traditions. The Teatro Popular was about provoking social change among the poor and disenfranchised (Ribadeneira 122).

With the return to a democratic government in 1966, new policies and priorities brought Paccioni's work to a close. His immediate legacy, however, produced the Escuela de Teatro de la Casa de la Cultura Ecuatoriana (The Ecuadorian House of Culture's School of Theater). This school was Ecuador's first formal effort to cultivate theater. Although it did not offer official degrees and titles, it did have a structured curriculum and a talented corps of instructors who taught approximately 100 students. Several of the participants became instrumental in creating new theater groups in Ecuador.

Notwithstanding Paccioni's success with the Teatro Ensayo and the Teatro Popular, and the subsequent creation of the Escuela de Teatro, the apparent progress that had been made was not sustained. By the end of the 1970s, Ecuadorian theater was as fragile and disconnected as it had always been. Even at the close of the twentieth century, theater groups continue to come and go like the proverbial ships that pass in the night. Clearly, there is no coherent plan or agenda from which to build; furthermore, with few exceptions, neither the private nor the public sector has truly concerned itself with providing an institutional structure that might consolidate and cultivate theater's dispersed talent and creativity. It is no wonder that Ecuadorian theater has been referred to as the performing arts' Cinderella (Campos 413).

DANCE

Although dance dates back to pre-Columbian times, as one of the performing arts it has fared no better than theater. The lack of continuity and the inability to develop a dance tradition from Ecuador's rich indigenous roots should not suggest a dearth of talent, however. In fact, as recently as May 1999, Ecuador had a choreography festival that attracted some 20 groups from throughout the country. Based on the performances presented at the festival, it is apparent that Ecuadorian dance has three predominant forms of expression: classical, modern, and a kind of *ballet folklórico* that re-creates Ecuador's many regional dances.

During the last half of the twentieth century, there have been numerous attempts to create a national form of dance that would combine classical and folk traditions. Efforts to realize this goal of artistic and cultural syncretism were reminiscent of those carried out by Ecuador's painters and musicians. Noralma Vera, for example, combined classical dance with regional costumes and props in several ballets she produced during the early 1960s at the House of Culture in Guayaquil.

The challenge, of course, was to create a holistic art form rather than a pastiche of disjointed movements devoid of an authentic cultural context. Wilson Pico was especially adept at producing innovative and culturally rel-evant forms of dance. His choreography incorporated body language and gestures that evoked experiences and situations characteristic of Ecuador's common folk.

As in so many other areas of Ecuadorian and Latin American culture, dance and its practitioners were energized by the ethos of the 1960s. The early experiments by Noralma Vera and Wilson Pico were among the first to attempt to create dance forms that were socially responsible. Like other art-ists, they understood the urgency of using artistic expression to raise the social consciousness of their audiences.

Social commitment was, indeed, at the heart of *Daquilema*, a choreo-graphed interpretation of the Ecuadorian Indian who led an unsuccessful uprising against oppressive landowners. Under the direction of the Chilean choreographer Germán Silva, dance became a means of revisiting historical events that had been forgotten or silenced. The *Daquilema* performance was especially significant because it was an interdisciplinary and multicultural effort that transcended traditional artistic and professional boundaries. It brought together the choreography created by Silva, the script prepared by José Félix Silva, the music arranged by Claudio Arízaga, the sets designed by Oswaldo Guayasamín, and the historical data provided by the anthropolo-gists Piedad and Alfredo Costales. More than 20 dancers interpreted the work.

Although *Daquilema* was a tour de force of innovation and creativity, it was criticized for being too stylized and contrived. The followers of Wilson Pico, for example, preferred less elaborate productions that came closer to capturing the grotesque and ugly conditions against which Ecuador's masses continued to struggle. This desire to establish greater proximity to Ecuador's oppressed peoples inspired numerous dancers and choreographers to perform in the public plazas and streets. Street performances were not just a means of taking dance directly to the people; they were an attempt to allow the street culture to influence the dancing (Solórzano and Rivadeneira 146).

With the oil boom of the 1970s, Ecuador's government earmarked some of its new resources to support dance education and performance. In 1974, it created the National Institute of Dance, which became part of the Ministry of Education and Culture. With the participation of accomplished foreign choreographers and dancers in a variety of sponsored programs, the quality of dance improved quickly. By 1976, the government created the National Dance Company in order to make dance more professional in Ecuador. In an environment of systematic training and discipline, the National Dance Company produced a cadre of outstanding choreographers and dancers who would take dance into the 1980s (Solórzano and Rivadeneira 147).

Unfortunately, much of the progress made in the 1970s was short-lived. A rising foreign debt and plummeting oil prices turned Ecuador's economic bonanza of the 1970s into a financial and social debacle. Without stable patronage, the dance community had to scramble to find new sponsors for its activities. Indeed, the financial struggle to survive virtually destroyed the previous decade's attempts to establish a coherent and consistent plan for the development of dance in Ecuador. Once again, dance groups found themselves dispersed, disconnected, and directionless (Solórzano and Rivadeneira 149).

The history of dance (as well as that of the other performing arts) is yet another example of Ecuador's national paradox. So much talent and so few opportunities! At the risk of sounding trite, it is tempting to describe Ecuador as a kind of Sleeping Beauty. That is not to suggest, however, that Ecuadorians are passively waiting for someone else to solve their problems. The accomplishments and ongoing efforts of such outstanding choreographers and dancers as Noralma Vera, Wilson Pico, Marcelo Ordóñez, Ingrid Bruckman, Luis Mueckay, and Isabel Bustos indicate the extent to which many Ecuadorians have struggled to be agents of change.

REFERENCES

Barrera, Isaac J. *Historia de la literatura Ecuatoriana*. Quito: Libresa, 1979.

Béhague, Gerard H. *Music and Black Ethnicity: The Caribbean and South America*. New Brunswick, NJ: Transaction Publishers, 1992.

Campos, Luis Miguel. "Actualidad del teatro Ecuatoriano en ocho puntos." In *La Literatura Ecuatoriana de las dos últimas décadas (1970–1990)*. Ed. Eliécer Cárdenas and María Eugenia Moscoso Carvalho. Cuenca: Universidad de Cuenca y Casa de la Cultura Ecuatoriana, 1993. 413–445.

Descalzi, Ricardo. "El Teatro en la vida republicana: 1830–1980." In *Arte y Cultura. Ecuador: 1830–1980*. Ed. Luis Mora Ortega. Quito: Corporación Editora Nacional, 1980. 349–358.

"Grupo de Danza Experimental Contemporánea." *Espejo*, 3, no. 4 (November 1981), 98–99.

Guerrero Gutiérrez, Pablo. *Músicos del Ecuador*. Quito: Corporación Musicológica Ecuatoriana, 1995.

———. "Tonos y bailes del Ecuador." In *Cantares: Cancionero de música Ecuatoriana*. Quito: CONMUSICA, 1997. 60–65.

Guevara, Gerardo. "La música en el Ecuador." *Espejo*, 5, no. 7 (April 1983), 46–53.

Luzuriaga, Gerardo. *Bibliografía del teatro Ecuatoriano, 1900–1982*. Quito: Casa de la Cultura Ecuatoriana, 1984.

Medina, Clara, ed. "Guayaquil y su teatro." *Semana gráfica del telégrafo* (27 July 1997), D1–D8.

Ribadeneira, Edmundo. "Reflexiones alrededor del teatro." In *Signos de futuro*. Ed. José Sánchez-Parga. Quito: Abya-Yala, 1991.

Rodas, Arturo. "Grandeza de Luis H. Salgado, miseria nuestra." *Palabra suelta*, 6 (1989), 60–61.

Sáenz A., Bruno. "Música y músicos recuperados." *Palabra suelta*, 1 (1987), 37–39.

San Félix, Alvaro. "Teatro: Pronóstico Reservado." *Espejo*, 1, no. 1 (March 1979), 24–28.

Santillán Peralbo, Rodrigo. "Los caminos de la danza." *Espejo*, 5, no. 7 (April 1983), 83–91.

Sigmund, Charles. "Segundo Luis Moreno (1882–1972), el primer musicólogo del Ecuador." *Cultura*, 4, no. 11 (September–December 1981), 265–294.

Solórzano, Laura, and Santiago Rivadeneira. "Ficción y realidad de la danza en el Ecuador." In *Signos de futuro*. Ed. José Sánchez-Parga. Quito: Abya-Yala, 1991. 141–158.

Vivanco, Jorge. "Malayerba ¿o los buenos frutos?" *Espejo*, 4, no. 6 (August 1982), 110–114.

8

Crafts, Painting, Sculpture, and Architecture

The arts have a rich history in Ecuador. By 3000 B.C., the Valdivia culture of the Pacific coast had developed advanced skills in ceramics. Archaeologists have uncovered exquisite figurines and jugs. Many of the pieces reveal a harmonious blending of the practical and the artistic. Besides each object's functional value for the daily tasks associated with food, work, and pleasure, the pieces expressed the human relationship to nature and to pre-Columbian deities. By means of the zoomorphic and anthropomorphic figures that adorn much of their ceramic ware and jewelry-like ornaments, Ecuador's early peoples clearly exhibited a propensity for creative and artistic interpretation of their social and cultural milieu. Their creativity and artistry were the foundation for future generations of artists and artisans in Ecuador.

LO POPULAR IN ECUADORIAN ART

The continuity of artistic traditions is especially evident in what is commonly referred to as *las artes populares* (the popular arts). In Spanish, *lo popular* is derived from *pueblo*, a term that generally refers to a nation's common people or "folk." Thus, references to *lo popular* have little to do with popularity; rather, they evoke what might be best expressed in English as "arts and crafts."

Many of today's artisans use the same materials and tools as their ancestors centuries ago. Furthermore, despite a long-standing Western bias against popular forms of art, one that has frequently categorized the latter as "folk art" rather than "art," a growing interest in cultural anthropology and ar-

Typical loom for weaving. Courtesy of James Minton.

chaeology that dates from about 1950 in Ecuador has brought to light the aesthetic and artistic value of popular art. In fact, rather than dichotomize artistic expression into "high" and "low" forms, many progressive thinkers have emphasized the connections between art's multiple forms of expression.

In Ecuador, the boundaries between artists and artisans have been more imagined than real. Just as the pre-Columbian cultures combined the practical and the artistic, so subsequent generations have cultivated art forms that have been characterized more by collaboration and the use of common sources than by isolation and separatism. Quito's extraordinary baroque churches of the seventeenth century, for example, were built and adorned by native craftsmen who, although directed by foreign architects and artists, frequently managed to leave behind their artistic imprint. Similarly, many modern painters and sculptors have incorporated into their work motifs and materials commonly used by Ecuador's artisans.

Symbolically, at least, 1982 was a watershed year for Ecuador's popular artists. The Organization of American States (OAS) declared that year to be "The Inter-American Year of Arts and Crafts." As in other Latin American countries, public and private institutions in Ecuador sponsored numerous exhibits, seminars, and workshops that featured many of the country's most skillful popular artists and their work. Unfortunately, limited resources did not provide for ongoing educational and cultural programs that could have offered the general public a comprehensive and penetrating understanding of the social and artistic value of Ecuador's arts and crafts (Dávila Vázquez 82).

Notwithstanding the mostly ceremonial nature of the official festivities of 1982, public awareness of the popular arts did increase to some degree. Besides discussions about the aesthetic merits of the popular art forms, there were attempts in some intellectual circles to define arts and crafts as a fundamental expression of the nation's unique cultural heritage and artistic patrimony. In that regard, knowledgeable initiates and aficionados brought to light the social and economic conditions that threatened to destroy or distort many of Ecuador's artistic traditions.

Rapidly changing lifestyles as a result of modern-day market forces and production patterns have made it increasingly difficult for popular artists to continue cultivating their work. Mass production and the use of plastic instead of clay, for example, have threatened the future of those who create elaborate designs that for centuries have adorned so much of Ecuador's pottery, leather work, and jewelry. Similarly, intricate wood carvings and beautiful embroidery that preserve motifs and techniques passed from generation to generation stubbornly await buyers who resist the allure of machine-made replicas devoid of the cultural and historical content that characterizes the handmade originals.

It is impossible to predict the future of Ecuador's *artes populares*, particularly in light of the market pressures that are inherent in today's consumer society. Nevertheless, throughout Ecuador, there are still artisans who have managed to survive and to preserve their artistic traditions. In fact, a visit to Cuenca, Ibarra, or Otavalo—three centers that have long been famous for their arts and crafts—is like entering a kind of time warp where centuries of accumulated knowledge, skill, and artistry are vibrantly evident to the careful observer.

THE QUITO SCHOOL AND COLONIAL ART

In addition to its *artes populares*, Ecuador has long been one of America's principal centers of colonial art. The fundamental corpus of colonial art was almost exclusively religious. Between the sixteenth and early nineteenth centuries, the dominant school of painting, sculpture, and architecture was sponsored and cultivated by the Catholic Church. Thus, religious themes prevailed, especially in Quito, which had become the hub for most of the church's ecclesiastical, educational, and cultural activities.

Shortly after the Spanish conquest in 1532, the church initiated its evangelical conquest and conversion of the region's indigenous peoples. As was the case throughout Latin America, in Ecuador the church frequently utilized art and architecture as a means of proselytizing and of establishing itself as the supreme authority in religious matters. The architecture of each church—massive, beautifully adorned, and centrally located—symbolized the institution's absolute power. Likewise, the huge and elaborate paintings and sculptures that filled the churches were intended to re-create the glory and omnipresence of God's pantheon of triumphant disciples, saints, and martyrs.

One could certainly question the church's use and abuse of power during the colonial period. However, the epic proportions and the magnificence of its evangelical project as expressed through the arts are undeniable. With the exception of some paintings and sculptures brought to America from Europe, the overwhelming body of artistic and architectural work associated with the church in Ecuador (and in much of Latin America) was carried out in the colonies by indigenous local artisans and workers. In less than 200 years, the church had succeeded in establishing an elaborate system that transplanted and reproduced the European Renaissance in the Americas.

The convents, missions, cloisters, churches, and cathedrals that sprang up were veritable museums of art (Barrera 224). Quito became known as a city of church domes and bell towers. By the seventeenth century, it was filled with such sumptuous baroque structures as the Saint Francis Church and monastery, the cathedral, the Sanctuary of Guápulo, the Company of Jesus, and the religious order of *La Merced*. Each of these structures was laden with sculpted and hand-carved religious images that adorned altars and pulpits. Together, they continue to represent a live testimony of one of Ecuador's principal Golden Ages of art—*la Escuela Quiteña* (The Quito School of Art).

Because the church was the principal patron and sponsor of the arts throughout Latin America during the colonial period, its religious agenda influenced much of the art that was produced. Not surprisingly, the recurring religious themes and symbols that transcended geographic borders have made it extremely difficult to distinguish national artistic themes, styles, and techniques. Thus, some critics have questioned whether there really was a unique artistic school or style commonly called the *Escuela Quiteña*. Be that as it may, for more than three centuries Quito was a thriving center for religious art where training and production were abundant and uninterrupted (Barrera 224).

The beginnings of the Quito School can be traced to Jodoco Ricke, the first Franciscan friar to arrive in Quito (1534). He immediately founded the Saint Francis convent, and in 1537, he initiated the construction of the Saint

Francis Church and monastery, which were finally completed in 1686. In 1551, in collaboration with Pedro Gosseal, another Franciscan, Ricke founded the first school of arts and crafts in the Americas which, in 1556, was named the Colegio San Andrés (St. Andrew School).

Originally, Ricke and Gosseal taught their painting skills primarily to Indians and to some mestizos; later, as the school grew, most of the teachers and apprentices were mestizos (Kennedy Troya and Ortiz Crespo, "Reflexiones sobre el arte colonial quiteño" 169–170). Many native painters learned to copy and imitate European works, especially those from Spain. Eventually, other European painters joined Ricke and Gosseal in Quito to further the arts among local artisans. Moreover, as the church brought to Quito some of Europe's finest paintings to adorn its buildings, these models helped raise the quality of artistic (re)production (Barrera 224).

Notwithstanding the obvious European influences that characterized much of the religious art produced in Quito beginning in the 1550s, it would be an error to underestimate the contributions made by local painters and artisans. Some have argued that the paints and surfaces used for the artwork were unique to Ecuador (Barrera 224). Others have pointed out that many of the images and depictions of religious figures and scenes evoke an Ecuadorian atmosphere more than a European one. Instead of the grapevines so prevalent in European Renaissance painting, for example, many of the altars and pulpits in Quito's churches were adorned with papayas and avocados (Rodríguez 43–44).

From its inception, the school of arts and crafts founded by Ricke and Gosseal was Ecuador's principal learning center for religious painting, sculpture, and architecture. At the same time, the myriad churches constructed during the colonial era required a constant supply of trained artists and artisans. By the sixteenth century, the school had established a wide network of artists and artisans whose work was an overwhelming presence in colonial Ecuador.

Despite the anonymity of the vast majority of painters, sculptors, and craftsmen who made up the workforce of the *Escuela Quiteña*, several individuals emerged in the seventeenth and eighteenth centuries as leading figures who embodied the very best of colonial art. Miguel de Santiago, for example, is considered by some to be Spanish America's best painter of the seventeenth century. Born in Quito in 1630, he produced paintings, over a span of some fifty years, that expressed the passion and suffering of Jesus with rare religious fervor (Rodríguez 44). According to legend, on one occasion Santiago was so intent upon capturing the agony Christ had experienced at the time of his crucifixion that he plunged a stake into the heart of the youngster who was posing for him. Observing the model's suffering in his last moments of life, Santiago was supposedly ecstatic as he transposed to his canvas the *Agony of Christ* (Barrera 229).

Santiago's most famous disciple was the mestizo painter Nicolás Xavier de Goríbar. In addition to his many paintings of floating angels, the Virgin Mary, and Jesus, Goríbar was noted especially for his series of paintings titled *The Prophets*. Like his master, Goríbar was renowned for the pain and sorrow that he captured so vividly in his religious paintings. Some of the works by Santiago and Goríbar are still in the same churches in Quito where they were first placed in the seventeenth century (e.g., Saint Augustine, Guápulo, and the cathedral).

Among the *Escuela Quiteña*'s most famous sculptors were Bernardo de Legarda and Manuel Chili, an Indian commonly referred to as Caspicara (Wooden Face). Legarda was born at the end of the seventeenth century in Quito, and was known primarily for his wood carvings and paintings. His masterpiece was the 1736 carving *Virgin of the Apocalypse*, which is better known as the *Winged Virgin of Quito*. This work is especially noteworthy for the mystical aura that emerges from the twisting figure of the Virgin, who, with arms spread like wings, tramples the head of a dragon. Unlike the fair-skinned European Virgins, she clearly has the facial features and coloring of a mestiza.

The work of Caspicara was discovered in 1791 by Eugenio Espejo, Ecuador's leading intellectual of the late eighteenth century. Caspicara was an outstanding sculptor of religious images in polychromed wood. His work was characterized by his knowledge of the human body and an impeccable technique of representation. Among his most famous works (the exact dates are unknown) are the *Four Virtues* and the *Holy Shroud*, both of which are in Quito's cathedral. Of equal importance are his *Saint Francis, The Twelve Apostles*, and the *Assumption of the Virgin*, all of which are in the Church of Saint Francis. Art critics have often marveled at Caspicara's ability to group figures in ways that evoke painting as much as sculpture.

Manuel Samaniego was the *Escuela Quiteña*'s last outstanding artist. Born around 1767 in Quito, he painted frescoes of scenes from the life of Christ in collaboration with his teacher, Bernardo Rodríguez. These works are in the upper arches of the central nave in Quito's cathedral. In addition, Samaniego produced such masterpieces as *Death of the Virgin, Adoration of the Magi*, and *The Last Supper*. One of his favorite subjects was the Immaculate Conception. In general, Samaniego's painting style was characterized by a serenity perhaps produced by his penchant for using shades of blue.

The Escuela Quiteña and Cultural Patrimony

The artistic quality and historical significance of the *Escuela Quiteña* are very much alive. Since 1975, there has been a resurgence of interest in evaluating and preserving its legacy. After it was officially acknowledged during that year as part of Ecuador's cultural patrimony that is at risk of disappearing due to neglect and profiteering, teams of artists and artisans initiated a long-term preservation project. On the one hand, ongoing efforts are being made to clean and restore works that have deteriorated through the centuries. At the same time, an all-out campaign is being waged against those who would smuggle works of art out of the country and sell them on the international market.

NINETEENTH-CENTURY PAINTING AND PAINTERS

Although painters continued working within the tradition of the *Escuela Quiteña* well into the nineteenth century, Manuel Samaniego's death in 1824 signaled, for all practical purposes, the end of Ecuador's Golden Age of religious art—at least its creative phase. With independence in 1822, a new mind-set arose among Ecuadorians. In place of the religious fervor that had been so characteristic of the colonial period, nineteenth-century military campaigns and war heroes, for example, created a keen interest in more worldly matters. This change was reflected in painting.

Portrait painting was one of the first artistic forms that signaled the coming of a new age. The transition, of course, was gradual. By the late eighteenth century, Ecuador's intelligentsia was focusing more attention on its natural surroundings. The growing importance of the natural sciences, in particular, was largely responsible for challenging the dominance of religion and the church in everyday life. Moreover, as the revolutionary spirit and the desire for independence from Spain evolved, civic affairs began to occupy a more central place in society than had been the case in the past.

Consequently, it was logical for painters to look beyond traditional biblical themes for their inspiration. Not only did early national heroes and military leaders emerge as worthy subjects, but so, too, did members of the ruling elites who had the wherewithal to commission their portraits. On the surface, at least, the popularity of portrait painting seemed to suggest two things: first, overt self-indulgence had become acceptable social behavior among the wealthy; and second, a growing sense of the individual's own importance had displaced earlier manifestations of piety and humility.

Gaspar Sangurima of Cuenca was Ecuador's first noteworthy portrait painter. In 1822, he presented Simón Bolívar with a portrait as a gift to celebrate independence and the liberator's heroic deeds. Bolívar was so impressed with the gesture and the quality of the painting that he decreed that Cuenca have its first official school of fine arts. He named Sangurima as the school's director, who would train thirty youngsters in painting, sculpture, architecture, carpentry, watchmaking, and silverwork (Vargas 423–424). Sangurima's studio and workshop trained a generation of accomplished artists and artisans in Cuenca during the nineteenth century.

Antonio Salas (1780–1860) established portrait painting as a legitimate genre in Ecuador. In 1824, Juan José Flores, one of Bolívar's leading generals, who became Ecuador's first president in 1830, commissioned Salas to paint the portraits of 22 military officials. Such an assignment clearly exemplifies the extent to which social values and mores had changed since colonial times (Vargas 425). Furthermore, whereas the church had been the principal patron of earlier artists and artisans, independence and a civil government meant the rise of a new institution that would cultivate the arts according to its political objectives and interests.

In 1852, the government created the Escuela Democrática Miguel de Santiago (the Miguel de Santiago Democratic School). This school was the precursor of the School of Fine Arts created in 1872 by President Gabriel García Moreno. This academic center offered instruction in painting, sculpture, and architecture. Initially, García Moreno had sent a group of young artists to Italy so they could develop their talents and come home as teachers. Upon their return, and with the addition of foreign teachers, the government was able to launch its project. Unfortunately, following García Moreno's death in 1875, the School of Fine Arts disbanded; it did not reopen until the government of General Leonidas Plaza reorganized it in 1904. Since that time, almost every outstanding Ecuadorian artist has had some affiliation with the school (Vargas 429).

Because the nineteenth century was a period of nation building and intense nationalism in Europe and Latin America, painting evolved as an essential means of representing each country's uniqueness. Indeed, besides the portraits of public figures and ruling elites that marked the early years of independence, Ecuador itself became the predominant theme in the arts. Landscape painting and *costumbrismo* (a genre that portrays everyday life and prevailing customs) played a decisive role in Ecuador's national project.

The interest in capturing Ecuadorian scenery and geography through art was inspired in no small measure by two foreign scientists who had arrived in 1871 to study Ecuador's mountains and volcanoes. Alphons Stübel and Wilhelm Reiss hired the young Ecuadorian painter Rafael Troya to illustrate their scientific findings for each mountain. With this experience, Troya discovered landscape painting as a bona fide genre for his own artistic work. More important, the formal attention that he gave to depicting Ecuador's physical setting opened up a new chapter in the history of Ecuadorian art (Vargas 428).

Troya's paintings complemented the *costumbrista* works that some of his peers had been developing since the middle of the century. Joaquín Pinto, Juan Manosalvas, and Rafael Salas were especially adept at using watercolors to portray Ecuador's social landscape. The common man's physical characteristics, his gestures, and his daily activities became favorite subjects for the *costumbristas*. The earlier portrait subjects insisted that they were European and cosmopolitan—at least insofar as their race and culture were concerned. The masses (or *pueblo*), on the other hand, were seen as the true embodiment of Ecuador's authenticity and uniqueness vis-à-vis the rest of the world.

Unfortunately, the depiction of the common folk rarely amounted to much more than a symbolic portrait of the nation. The *costumbristas* generally did not offer a critical or analytical view of Ecuador's *pueblo* (Castro y Velázquez 472). Rather, their search for essential qualities and human types led to a sanitized version of the nation. Stereotypes prevailed in a society that was intent upon creating a unified and harmonious nation.

Because foreign tourists and diplomats were the most enthusiastic purchasers of *costumbrista* art, one can only guess to what extent consumer preferences and attitudes influenced the content of Ecuador's *costumbrismo*. One could argue that competing objectives were at the heart of much of Ecuador's nineteenth-century painting. On the one hand, the need to represent the newly founded nation accurately inspired artists to turn their attention to Ecuador's physical and cultural features. On the other hand, the pressure to generate interest among wealthy outsiders may have skewed Ecuador's national portrait. Be that as it may, a definite ambivalence seems to run through Ecuadorian *costumbrismo*. Minute details and exactness are juxtaposed with an idealized view of nineteenth-century Ecuador (Castro y Velázquez 473).

The artistic treatment of Ecuador's Indians is a perfect example of the contradiction described above. *Costumbrista* painters were instrumental in depicting many of the social habits and mores that characterized the country's indigenous communities (Vargas 428). In some ways, the body of *costumbrista* painting constituted a kind of ethnography that previously had been absent from the arts in Ecuador. At the same time, however, no reference was made to the stark social conditions or general suffering that marked the Indians' place in society. This dark side of the national portrait did not appear until the twentieth-century.

TWENTIETH-CENTURY PAINTING AND SOCIAL REALISM

The end of the nineteenth century was a tumultuous period in Ecuadorian history. With the Liberal Revolution of 1895, Ecuador became a more democratic and pluralistic society. Social justice and civil rights were at the heart of the new government's attempts to erase the privileges traditionally enjoyed by the oligarchy and the Catholic Church. Indeed, the adoption of new laws and the creation of new institutions politicized every aspect of life in Ecuador.

To the extent that the arts are a product of their social and historical milieu, it is no wonder that the descriptive and highly decorative nature of nineteenth-century *costumbrismo* and portrait painting was replaced by a style consistent with the changing times. At the beginning of the twentieth century, artists began to look deeper and more critically into the Ecuadorian landscape. Whereas in previous generations artists had set out to please audiences, by means of inspirational religious figures or reassuring scenes of bliss, innocence, and beauty, twentieth-century painters shocked their viewers with dark colors and contorted images of pain and suffering. For all practical purposes, by 1930 art had become a vehicle for protest and social change.

Many social and historical events greatly influenced Ecuador's artists of the modern period (e.g., Ecuador's Liberal Revolution, the Mexican Revolution, the Russian Revolution, World War I). However, twentieth-century art was not merely a product of politics and social conflict. German expressionism, which emphasized emotion through the distortion of line, shape, and color, and Mexican muralism also played a vital role in determining the new directions that Ecuadorian art would take, especially during the first half of the twentieth century. Mexican muralists such as Diego Rivera, David Siqueiros, and José Clemente Orozco championed a form of public art that would be fundamental to the "search for national and cultural identity" which characterized so many Latin American countries, including Ecuador (Lucie-Smith 19). Whereas German expressionism was noted for interpreting the individual's anguished cry against loneliness and despair, Mexican muralism celebrated a people's struggle to forge a new national destiny (Debray 34).

By combining the basic features of expressionism and muralism, Ecuadorian artists created their own unique style of social realism. The plight of

Ecuador's marginalized and forgotten masses became the heart and soul of twentieth-century painting. Each portrait of the country's Indians, peasants, and urban poor was a public condemnation of the horrors of poverty, exploitation, and injustice. Just as the period's writers had done in literature, Ecuador's social realist painters had embarked upon a project that was tantamount to reconstructing the national image. The sterile and vacuous representations of the *pueblo* common to so many *costumbrista* paintings were displaced by subjects that seemed to cry out for public recognition and sweeping change.

It is not surprising that Indians became the predominant theme in much of Ecuador's social realist painting. They constituted by far the largest segment of Ecuador's population, and their history had to be fundamental to any viable concept of the nation. However, with the publication of *Huasipungo* in 1934, the novel in which Jorge Icaza unmasked four centuries of physical and psychological brutality, Ecuadorians were challenged to confront their heritage openly and honestly. Consequently, in contrast to the nationalistic rhetoric that extolled the country's glorious Inca past, Ecuador's painters took up Icaza's clarion call to mirror the cancer, exemplified by the Indian experience, that continued to corrupt every aspect of their society.

The social protest that was so evident in social realist painting was not just about helpless victims. A definite sense of defiance runs through much of the work. Also, there was fluidity between expressionist and muralist influences. Some of the most memorable works painted in the first half of the twentieth century brought to life a complex of contradictory emotions and perspectives that would define Ecuador as a country of "drama and paradox" (Benites Vinueza 277). Indeed, the stereotypical and cardboard characters of the previous century had given way to a people whose clenched fists symbolized both the anguish that had been suffered during 400 years of servitude and the rebelliousness that had made possible their survival.

Camilo Egas as Precursor

One of the most important artists who helped to bridge the nineteenth and twentieth centuries was Camilo Egas (1889–1962). Although one might argue that Egas's early experiments with dark chromatic tones and distorted images were modest and restrained, his paintings were more sober than those of the *costumbristas*. In fact, by 1918, Egas had established himself as a precursor of Ecuadorian *indigenismo*, a term generally used to identify the movement of social protest that championed Indian rights throughout Latin America, especially in the 1930s (Rodríguez Castelo 114).

Beginning in 1927, Egas spent about a decade in New York, where he fully evolved as an expressionist painter. The Great Depression profoundly influenced both his view of life and his painting style. One of Egas's most memorable works from this period was his 1937 painting *La calle 14* (14th Street). In it, he depicts a stark and lonely scene in a New York subway station. The principal character shivers in the winter cold; his bald head, blank stare, crossed arms, and crouched body capture the tragedy of a man who is unprotected and friendless (Rodríguez Castelo 114).

Upon his return to Ecuador, Egas became an influential proponent of the social and expressionist styles that have become the unique mark of modern Ecuadorian painting. By the 1940s, however, Egas began to experiment with neocubism and numerous abstract styles that gave his work a powerful visual quality. It has been said that through his career, Egas came to understand that art was most effective when it was suggestive rather than mimetic. Thus, one can understand his fascination with the novel use of symbols and unorthodox images. Egas's final works were a mature synthesis of his constant search for new techniques and his many artistic experiments (Rodríguez Castelo 114). More important, Egas's latter period is a poignant reminder of how innovative and dynamic many of Ecuador's artists have been throughout the twentieth century.

Eduardo Kingman and the Muralist Tradition

Although there are a host of outstanding artists in twentieth-century Ecuador, Eduardo Kingman is undoubtedly one of the country's two or three true giants. Born in 1913, he has received numerous prizes and awards for his work; over the years, he has had many exhibits in Ecuador, Colombia, Venezuela, the United States, France, and Russia. He has many talents: painter, draftsmen, engraver, and muralist. His principal claim to fame is probably as Ecuador's first important muralist (Lucie-Smith 69). Kingman emerged on the art scene during New York's 1939 World's Fair, where he won first prize in the mural competition.

Profoundly influenced by the Mexican muralist Diego Rivera, Kingman focused his artistic energies on portraying Ecuador's Indians. Not surprisingly, much of his work has been fundamental in defining the basic qualities of social realist painting in Ecuador. Notwithstanding the many traits that Kingman shares with other artists, his work is unmistakably unique. Kingman is noted for the prominence of his subjects' hands. They come in all shapes and sizes, and even a cursory review of Kingman's work leaves a haunting impression. The hands are symbolic of four centuries of toil and labor; in Kingman, they define the history and culture of a people.

One of Kingman's most revered masterpieces is the 1941 painting *Los Guandos* (Loads of Freight). Part of Ecuadorian trade practices in the past was the transporting of heavy loads of freight between the Coast and the Sierra. It was the Indians who generally carried the loads on litters. As Kingman shows in his painting, some of the loads were so huge that groups of six or more were necessary to transport them. Under the watchful eye and quick whip of a foreman on horseback, teams of Indians struggled to keep moving. Not only does Kingman narrate the nightmare of forced labor, but he also captures the horror of a society that allowed Indians to be (ab)used as beasts of burden. Each contorted face tells a unique story: some are numb with pain, others are beaten by exhaustion, and still others reveal clenched jaws of anger and rebellion.

Los Guandos includes Kingman's famous hands. In stark contrast to the painting's sense of fatigue and suffering, the large, thick hands with long fingers appear to emphasize the Indian's strength and resilience. Indeed, they are an affirmation of life.

Kingman's legacy to Ecuadorian art has extended beyond his paintings. He has spent years as a teacher and promoter of art. When he returned to Quito in 1940, shortly after the New York World's Fair, he founded the Caspicara Art Gallery "which became a center for progressive artistic activity" (Lucie-Smith 70). Later in the decade, after serving briefly on the staff of the San Francisco Museum of Art, Kingman again returned home. In 1947, he became the director of Ecuador's National Museum and the National Artistic Heritage (Lucie-Smith 70).

The Monumentalism of Oswaldo Guayasamín

Oswaldo Guayasamín (1919–1999) is Ecuador's most internationally recognized artist of all time. His murals are in Quito, Caracas, and Madrid; he has had exhibits throughout Latin America, the United States, and Western and Eastern Europe. Among his most notable prizes and awards was the one he received in São Paulo, Brazil, which named him South America's best painter in 1957. In general, Guayasamín's work has been described as a cross between Picasso and the Mexican muralist José Clemente Orozco (Chase 114). Like many great artists, Guayasamín was both prolific and multifaceted; his work evolved in many different directions over more than half a century.

Although Guayasamín had much in common with Eduardo Kingman, especially with regard to their contributions to social realist painting, Kingman's work never attained the breadth and the abundance that characterize Guayasamín's body of work. Aside from the stylistic and technical features that have given Guayasamín's work its uniqueness, the most salient quality is its monumentalism. His hundreds of paintings together offer a coherent and organic view of life in Ecuador, Latin America, and the world in general.

Guayasamín's first important period began in the late 1930s, when he was fully engaged in the social realist movement. Much of his early work was conceived as an overt protest against the emotional and physical suffering of the Indians. The dark tones that he used to express the Indian experience as a kind of national saga were consistent with the expressionist style that had become so influential in Ecuadorian painting.

A second stage in Guayasamín's evolution is generally identified with his first monumental project, *Huaycañán*, a Quichua word that means "the Road of Tears." This series of 100 paintings was completed in 1952; it was basically an interpretation of the suffering that characterized Ecuador's Indians, Blacks, and mestizos. The racial variety of his subjects allowed Guayasamín to experiment with a diversity of colors that were absent from his previous work (Rodríguez Castelo 148). Furthermore, *Huaycañán* revealed a growing fascination with geometric forms reminiscent of cubist painting.

Huaycañán took the art world by storm. In 1956, Guayasamín received the Grand Prize at Barcelona's Spanish American Biennial Art Exhibit for one of the collection's triptychs, *El ataúd blanco* (The White Casket). From that point on, Guayasamín was recognized as one of Latin America's artistic geniuses.

Despite his success, Guayasamín did not rest on his laurels. He broadened his interests from national concerns to more universal ones. His second massive project, *La edad de la ira* (The Age of Wrath) initiated a new period in his career. This collection of 250 paintings narrated the tragedy of contemporary man. Like a novel, *La edad de la ira* was divided into chapterlike segments that captured the multiple causes and effects of injustice. For example, the paintings included in *Los campos de concentración* (The Concentration Camps) and *Mujeres ilorando* (Crying Women) depicted suffering and anger, while those in *Reunión en el Pentágono* (Meeting at the Pentagon) were a grotesque caricature of the world's international power structure.

Throughout the entire collection Guayasamín brought to life disconcerting images of pain, fear, terror, and sadness (Mora 185). Thin, cadaverous faces, skeleton-like bodies, and deformed hands express Guayasamín's wrath. It is not surprising that he has described his overall artistic production as an attempt to provoke anger: *"pintar para indignar"* (Oña, "Arte y nación en el Ecuador contemporáneo" 35). It is equally unsurprising that the political nature of much of his work made Guayasamín a highly controversial figure. Because he was an ardent supporter of the Cuban Revolution and other national liberation movements, it is often difficult to discern whether Guayasamín's critics are referring to his paintings or to his politics (Rodríguez Castelo 149).

It would be a mistake, however, to define Guayasamín only in terms of his social protest painting. Indeed, his multifaceted work is rich with examples of love and tenderness, even amid the pain that cries out from his canvases. Such is the case with his third project, *Mientras viva te recordaré* (As long as I Live, I Shall Remember You). Guayasamín dedicated this series to his mother and to the love that she inspired. In contrast to the two previous projects, it has been suggested that these works should be entitled "The Age of Tenderness" (Flores 215).

Shortly before his death in 1999, Guayasamín had launched his last major project. He conceived, designed, and supervised the construction in Quito of the Capilla del Hombre (Chapel of Man). This chapel, albeit incomplete, is poignant evidence of Guayasamín's legacy to the world. Upon posthumous completion, the chapel and the paintings it will eventually hold will be both a celebration of man's potential for decency and an affirmation of Guayasamín's belief that one day there will be justice and freedom for all.

Beyond Social Realist Painting

Guayasamín, Kingman, and other accomplished social realist painters would seem to embody Ecuadorian art of the twentieth century. However, many younger painters who began to produce their work after 1950 brought to Ecuador a variety of styles and techniques that have allowed the nation's art to evolve in many different directions. Of course, change did not come easily. Just as younger writers had great difficulty breaking with the canonized models of social realism of the 1930s, so artists struggled to forge their own niche of creativity and originality.

Attempts to reject social realist models were often seen as indifference to social justice, the cause célèbre that had inspired the previous generation of painters. The notion that Ecuadorian art had become static, repetitive, and lifeless was likened to a form of heterodoxy by many Ecuadorians (Mejía, "La pintura abstracta y neofigurativa . . ." 483). The allure of abstract art, for example, seemed to undermine the artist's role as a champion of Ecuador's poor and destitute. The challenge, then, was to experiment with new forms without distancing oneself from the national context.

Ecuador's new generation of artists responded to this challenge by returning to their popular roots. Traditional artisans were a source of artistic styles
and techniques that formed the basis for the emergence of a primitive or pre-
Columbianist school of art. As artists experimented with geometric shapes,
decorative motifs, and spatial relationships between objects, they began to
incorporate into their works many of the designs and forms that had long
been used by Ecuador's potters and weavers, for example. Especially noteworthy in this artistic vein were Enrique Tábara, Araceli Gilbert, Judith
Gutiérrez, Aníbal Villacís, and Estuardo Maldonado.

Collages with rag dolls, primitive masks, ceremonial objects, indigenous
icons, and unique combinations of tropical colors reflect the dynamic interaction between popular art and a more sophisticated art that characterizes
much of upper-class urban Ecuador. Unlike their European or North American counterparts, Ecuadorian artists are immersed in a multicultural and
plurinational society where cultural practices from diverse time periods co-
exist. Indeed, the bonds between cultures are strong, and therefore Ecuadorian primitivism as expressed in art "becomes charged with special meanings"
(Lucie-Smith 20) that have little to do with exoticism or escapism. The
juxtaposition of the primitive and the modern is natural and harmonious in
Ecuadorian contemporary art.

SCULPTURE

Although critics and art enthusiasts have written relatively little about
Ecuadorian sculpture, it has had many excellent practitioners, especially under the tutelage of the church during the colonial period. Much of Ecuadorian sculpture has been produced by anonymous artisans and artists. This
anonymity is clearly reflected in Ecuador's many heavily adorned church
altars and façades. In some ways, the legion of unknown sculptors may have
made it difficult to treat Ecuadorian sculpture as an identifiable body of work.

The loss of power by the church at the end of the nineteenth century
adversely affected the development of sculpture. Secular and private groups
generally did not promote ambitious projects in sculpture. Moreover, without sponsors, most sculptors could not afford to practice their art with any
meaningful degree of continuity. Materials were too expensive, and potential
buyers were too few to justify the required effort.

Periods of economic growth have helped to offset the void left by a weakened church. The cacao, banana, and oil booms benefited all of the arts,
particularly sculpture. Public monuments and murals have been an important
outlet for Ecuador's sculptors during the twentieth century. Perhaps the most

Cathedrals are at the center of Ecuadorian architecture. Courtesy of James Minton.

important sculptor is Jaime Andrade Moscoso (1913), who has worked in stone, metal, and wood. The most acclaimed of his stone murals are in Quito at the Central University, the Mariscal Sucre Airport, the Central Bank, and the Hotel Colón.

ARCHITECTURE

Ecuador does not have a great deal of the majestic pre-Columbian architecture that is so common in Mexico, Guatemala, and Peru. At the time of the Conquest, the Incas had not ruled long enough in Ecuador to launch major construction projects. Thus, Ecuadorian architecture did not dominate the natural landscape until the Catholic Church began building its massive and elaborate cathedrals, convents, and monasteries in the sixteenth and seventeenth centuries.

With the exception of the baroque façades and elaborate stone columns that adorn so many of Ecuador's churches, Ecuadorian colonial architecture was quite modest and unpretentious. Instead of palaces and mansions, the enclosed house with an interior patio was the predominant structure of the period. This was especially true in the principal Andean highland cities like

Bamboo huts on stilts are common dwellings in rural areas along the Coast. Courtesy of James Hilty.

Quito. The patio, which often had a central fountain and a full array of flowers, constituted one of the most overt expressions of colonial society's preference for privacy. In fact, the patio was so basic to colonial life that people often refer to the joke about the homeowner who instructed his architect to build a huge patio, and if there was space left over, to add some rooms (Salvat and Crespo, *Historia del arte ecuatoriano*, vol. 2, 130).

Because of Ecuador's diverse geography and varied climate, its architecture has long been characterized by deeply rooted regional styles. Building materials are an obvious source of the architectural differences. Depending upon the location, traditional houses were made principally from stone, wood, or bamboo. Unlike the Andean home, which was a kind of retreat, many of the Coastal homes reflected a more outgoing lifestyle. For example, huge windows with wooden shutters that open toward the street dominated the exterior of most buildings. This combination of windows and shutters provided both shade and a comfortable airflow for people to keep cool in a tropical climate (Salvat and Crespo, *Historia del arte ecuatoriano*, vol. 2, 139).

Traditional architecture is more likely to have been conserved in the highlands than along the Coast. Although all regions have been equally vulnerable to such disasters as earthquakes and fires, building materials used in the highlands have been more durable and more plentiful than those used on the Coast. Because of a history of catastrophic fires and the almost total destruction of forests in Ecuador, the extensive use of precious woods in colonial Guayaquil, for example, has been all but replaced by concrete (Salvat and Crespo, *Arte contemporáneo de Ecuador*, 92).

Generally speaking, a discussion of Ecuadorian contemporary architecture will necessarily center on the two major urban centers, Quito and Guayaquil. Contemporary architecture in Quito and Guayaquil is very similar to what one would expect to find in any major city. Ultramodern hotels, high-rise office buildings, elaborate shopping malls, bridges, and overpasses abound in both. Since the oil boom of the 1970s, each city has experienced major population growth that has been accompanied by massive construction projects. Quito has been very conscientious about maintaining an architectural symmetry that is based on its colonial roots. White stucco walls and red tile roofs give Quito its distinctive character.

Guayaquil has followed a very different architectural path. The lack of any coherent or systematic urban plan during the last half of the twentieth century has converted it into an architectural labyrinth. Bamboo shacks on hillsides overlook posh mansions with manicured lawns; concrete houses with zinc roofs stand in direct contrast to homes that evoke the suburban United States. The architectural disparities are ubiquitous in this city of more than 2 million people. Indeed, whereas Quito is a modern city with a definite colonial presence, Guayaquil is a postmodern mosaic where there are no boundaries between styles, be they lifestyles or architectural ones.

CONCLUSION

Ecuador's crafts, painting, sculpture, and architecture are deeply rooted in the country's social history. Unlike the limited circulation that continues to characterize written literature, the arts have reached massive audiences through the centuries. Moreover, they have been central to a host of projects intended to define the nation and its fundamental values. At times, the arts have been an instrument utilized by the powers that be; at other times, they have constituted a counterdiscourse that proclaimed the need for change and even revolution. Like other Latin Americans, many Ecuadorians have "consistently turned to . . . the visual arts to discover the real truths about themselves, truths for which they would have searched in vain elsewhere" (Lucie-Smith 8).

Guayaquil's Cathedral, in the French Gothic style.
Courtesy of James Minton.

REFERENCES

Almeida Reyes, Eduardo. *Monumentos arqueológicos del Ecuador.* Quito: Editora Luz de América, 1997.

Barrera, Isaac. *Historia de la literatura Ecuatoriana.* Quito: Libresa, 1979.

Benites Vinueza, Leopoldo. *Ecuador: Drama y paradoja.* Quito: Banco Central del Ecuador y Corporación Editora Nacional, 1986.

Castedo, Leopoldo. *Historia del arte Iberoamericano.* Madrid: Alianza Editorial, 1988.

Castro y Velázquez, Juan. "Un importante momento en la pintura Ecuatoriana: El costumbrismo." In *Arte y cultura Ecuador: 1830–1980.* Ed. Luis Mora Ortega. Quito: Corporación Editora Nacional, 1980. 469–473.

Chase, Gilbert. *Contemporary Art in Latin America.* New York: Free Press, 1970.

Dávila Vázquez, Jorge. "La supervivencia de la artesanía y sus problemas." *Espejo*, 4, no. 6 (August 1982), 82–88.

de la Torre Reyes, Carlos. "La pintura social en ciento cincuenta años de vida republicana." *In Arte y cultura. Ecuador: 1830–1980*. Ed. Luis Mora Ortega. Quito: Corporación Editora Nacional, 1980.

Debray, Régis, "Guayasamín en el Museo de Arte Moderno." *Espejo*, 3, no. 4 (November 1981), 32–36.

Flores, Inés María, ed. *100 artistas del Ecuador*. Quito: Dinediciones, 1992.

Kennedy Troya, Alexandra, and Alfonso Ortiz Crespo. "Continuismo colonial y cosmopolitismo en la arquitectura y el arte decimonónico Ecuatoriano." In *Nueva historia del Ecuador*. Vol. 8. Ed. Enrique Ayala Mora. Quito: Corporación Editora Nacional y Grijalbo, 1983. 119–139.

————. "Reflexiones sobre el Arte Colonial Quiteño. In *Nueva historia del Ecuador*. Vol. 5. Ed. Enrique Ayala Mora. Quito: Corporación Editora Nacional y Grijalbo, 1983. 163–185.

Lara, Jorge Salvador. *Breve historia contemporánea del Ecuador*. Mexico City: Fondo de Cultura Económica, 1995.

Lucie-Smith, Edward. *Latin American Art of the 20th Century*. London: Thames and Hudson, 1993.

Malo González, Claudio. "Las artes populares en ciento cincuenta años de vida republicana." In *Arte y cultura. Ecuador: 1830–1980*. Ed. Luis Mora Ortega. Quito: Corporación Editora Nacional, 1980. 433–442.

Mejía, Manuel Esteban. "El expresionismo: ¿Primer gran perfil de la plástica Ecuatoriana?" *Espejo*, 1, no. 1 (March 1979), 18–23.

————. "La pintura abstracta y neofigurativa en 150 Años de Vida Republiciana," in *Arte y cultura. Ecuador: 1830–1980*. Ed. Luis Mora Ortega. Quito: Corporación Editora Nacional, 1980.

Monteforte, Mario, ed. *Los signos del hombre*. Cuenca: Universidad Católica del Ecuador, 1985.

Mora, Alba Luz. *Tres intervenciones y crónica breve*. Quito: Editorial ENA, 1982.

Oña, Lenin. "Jaime Andrade Moscoso o el destino de la ecultura Ecuatoriana." *Palabra suelta*, 4 (1988), 31–34.

————. "Arte y Nación en el Ecuador contemporáneo." *Palabra suelta*, 7 (1989), 34–37.

Pareja Diezcanseco, Alfredo. *Historia de la República: El Ecuador desde 1830 a Nuestros días*. 2 vols. Guayaquil: Cromograph, 1974.

Rodríguez, Linda. "Patrimonio cultural: Un peligro conjurado." *Espejo*, 2, no. 3 (August 1980), 43–47.

Rodríguez, Castelo, Hernán. *Diccionario crítico de artistas plásticos del Ecuador del siglo XX*. Quito: Editorial Casa de la Cultura Ecuatoriana, 1992.

Salvat, Juan, and Eduardo Crespo, Eds. *Arte contemporáneo de Ecuador*. Quito: Salvat Editores, 1977.

————. *Historia del arte Ecuatoriano*. Vol 2. Quito: Salvat Editores, 1977.

Samaniego, Filoteo. "El retrato en el Ecuador." In *Arte y cultura. Ecuador: 1830–1980*. Ed. Luis Mora Ortega. Quito : Corporación Editora Nacional, 1980. 459–465.

Vargas, José María. "Visión Global de las artes plásticas en ciento cincuenta años de vida republicana." In *Arte y cultura. Ecuador: 1830–1980*. Ed. Luis Mora Ortega. Quito: Corporación Editora Nacional, 1980. 421–430.

Villacís Molina, Rodrigo. "El arte de la Colonia al siglo XIX." In *Nueva historia del Ecuador*. Vol 8. Ed. Enrique Ayala Mora. Quito: Corporación Editora Nacional y Grijalbo, 1983. 134–139.

Glossary

aji. A variety of red pepper used to season food; usually served in liquid form.

años viejos. Large puppet-like figures that evoke celebrities; people burn them on New Year's Eve to signal the end of the year.

artes populares. A general term that refers to the artistic expression of a country's common folk; it may often be translated as "arts and crafts."

chifa. A Chinese restaurant; may also refer to Chinese food.

cholo. A person of Indian and white ancestry who has adopted Western mores; often the term means "country bumpkin."

cine club. A group that meets regularly to watch and discuss movies.

cinemateca. Film library or archive.

compadrazgo. The relationship that exists between a child's parents and godparents.

fiesta rosada. The party that celebrates a girl's fifteenth birthday.

indianismo. A nineteenth-century artistic movement that was part of romanticism and idealized Indians as "noble savages."

indigenismo. A multifaceted movement of the twentieth century that was devoted to the defense of Indian rights in Latin America.

indor. A soccer game played with a small ball on a playing area that is smaller than a regulation field.

machismo. A complex term that emphasizes a man's ability to dominate his surroundings and other people.

mestizaje.   The racial and/or cultural fusion between Indians and whites.

pasillo.   Popular love song or ballad that evolved from the waltz.

plurinacionalidad.   A term used to describe Ecuador as a country made up of many nationalities; each nationality cultivates its unique traditions and heritage while remaining loyal to the Ecuadorian nation.

pueblo.   Aside from the general meaning of "town," this term often refers to the common people, or common folk, of a country.

quinceañera.   A girl who celebrates her fifteenth birthday; also, that celebration.

sanjuanito.   A festive and popular dance that combines Spanish and Indian musical traditions.

Selected Bibliography

Ayala Mora, Enrique. *Resumen de historia del Ecuador*. Quito: Corporación Editora Nacional, 1997.

Benites Vinueza, Leopoldo. *Ecuador: Drama y paradoja*. Quito: Banco Central del Ecuador y Corporación Editora Nacional, 1986.

Cueva, Agustín. *Entre la ira y la esperanza: Ensayos sobre la cultura nacional*. Cuenca: Editorial Casa de la Cultura Ecuatoriana, 1981.

Goffin, Alvin M. *The Rise of Protestant Evangelism in Ecuador, 1895–1990*. Gainesville: University Press of Florida, 1994.

Guerrero Gutiérrez, Pablo. *Músicos del Ecuador*. Quito: Corporación Musicológica Ecuatoriana, 1995.

Granda Noboa, Wilma. *Cine silente en Ecuador: 1895–1935*. Quito: Editorial Casa de la Cultura Ecuatoriana, 1995.

Handelsman, Michael. *Incursiones en el mundo literario del Ecuador*. Guayaquil: Universidad de Guayaquil, 1987.

———. *Lo afro y la plurinacionalidad: El caso Ecuatoriano visto desde su literatura*. Oxford, MS: Romance Monographs, 1999.

Harrison, Regina. *Signs, Songs, and Memory in the Andes: Translating Quechua Language and Culture*. Austin: University of Texas Press, 1989.

Lara, Jorge Salvador. *Breve historia contemporánea del Ecuador*. 2nd ed. Mexico City: Fondo de Cultura Económica, 1995.

Martz, John. *Ecuador: Conflicting Political Culture and the Quest for Progress*. Boston: Allyn and Bacon, 1972.

———. *Politics and Petroleum in Ecuador*. New Brunswick, NJ: Transaction Books, 1987.

Mora, Alba Luz. *La televisión en el Ecuador*. Guayaquil: Editorial Amauta, 1982.

Mora Ortega, Luis, ed. *Arte y cultura. Ecuador: 1830–1980*. Quito: Corporación Editora Nacional, 1980.

Rodríguez Castelo, Hernán. *Diccionario crítico de artistas plásticos del Ecuador del siglo XX.* Quito: Editorial Casa de la Cultura Ecuatoriana, 1992.

Salvat, Juan, and Eduardo Crespo, eds. *Arte contemporáneo de Ecuador.* Quito: Salvat Editores, 1977.

———. *Historia del arte Ecuatoriano.* 3 vols. Quito: Salvat Editores, 1977.

Sánchez-Parga, José, ed. *Signos de futuro.* Quito: Abya-Yala, 1991.

Waag, Michael. "The Ecuadorian Novel of the 1970s in the Context of Its Historical and Literary Past." Ph.D. diss., University of Illinois, 1983.

Whitten, Norman E. *Class, Kinship and Power in an Ecuadorian Town: The Negroes of San Lorenzo.* Stanford, CA: Stanford University Press, 1965.

Index

About the Author

MICHAEL HANDELSMAN is a Distinguished Professor of the Humanities at the University of Tennessee in Knoxville. He is the cofounder of the Asociacion de Ecuatorianistas, an international scholarly organization devoted to promoting Ecuadorian literature and culture outside of Ecuador. His research interests include Spanish-American prose, women writers, Afro-Hispanic literature, literary journals, and issues related to national identity.

LaVergne, TN USA
15 December 2010
208971LV00007B/1/P